Pitfalls

A Case for College Ministry

The Rev. Dr. Samson N. Gitau

AuthorHouse™
1663 Liberty Drive
Bloomington, IN 47403
www.authorhouse.com
Phone: 1-800-839-8640

© 2010 The Rev. Dr. Samson N. Gitau. All rights reserved.

No part of this book may be reproduced, stored in a retrieval system, or transmitted by any means without the written permission of the author.

First published by AuthorHouse 7/29/2010

ISBN: 978-1-4520-2686-2 (e)
ISBN: 978-1-4520-2685-5 (sc)

Library of Congress Control Number: 2010909249

Printed in the United States of America
Bloomington, Indiana

This book is printed on acid-free paper.

Table of Contents

Acknowledgements	ix
Chapter 1. Called to College Ministry	1
Chapter 2. Biblical Foundations for Ministry with Young Adults	11
Chapter 3. Models of Campus Ministry	37
Chapter 4. College Ministry Board	49
Chapter 5. College Ministry Programming	61
Chapter 6. Student Voices	119
Chapter 7. Leadership Recruitment Forum	133
Chapter 8. Barth House is Closed	141
Chapter 9. Evaluation of Barth House	179
Chapter 10. Reactions to Closure of Barth House	195
Chapter 11. Barth House is Sold	233
Chapter 12. References	257
Chapter 13. Biography	259

For Lily and Alex and for all college students seeking a deeper knowledge with God. May you find God coming to meet you and your quest realized.

Acknowledgements

It takes the efforts of many people to bring a book to publication. I will be ever grateful for the opportunity to serve as the director of college ministry in the Diocese of West Tennessee under the direction of Bishop Coleman and later under Bishop Don Johnson. My ministry would have been impossible without the sacrificial donation of the Gooch family from Grace/St. Luke's, who donated seed money, allowing the Diocese of West Tennessee to finance my position. Throughout my ten years of college ministry, I was blessed to have many cheerleaders, clergy friends, parishes and friends, who generously cheered me on with their moral, spiritual and financial support. My colleagues in college ministry at the University of Memphis, Rhodes College, and Christian Brothers were an inspiration and fun to work with. My most sincere thanks to many faculty, staff and administrators in all the four colleges I served, for their support in college ministry. But all this would have been impossible without the support of hundreds of students who participated in our programs and particularly those who provided much needed student leadership. My administrative assistants throughout these years: Elise Williams, Linda Clark, Debbie Herr, and Judy Clark, my organist, were of tremendous help in my ministry. My wife, Lilian, as always was most supportive in this ministry. So were our children: Nelly, Hosea and Gideon as they each studied for their college degrees at the University of Memphis. I cannot thank them enough for their help.

I am most grateful to Ms. Marian Smith and Ms. Pam M. Smith for kindly proofreading parts of this book and making helpful suggestions. However, I take full responsibility for the entire contents of this book including any typos or other mistakes that may still be found in it. It is my hope and prayer that my experience will be of help to college ministers and church leaders alike, as they explore ways and means of doing college ministry.

Chapter One

Called to College Ministry

*And I heard the voice of the Lord saying,
"Whom shall I send, and who will go for us?"
Then I said, "Here am I! Send me." (Isaiah 6:8)*

I love college ministry. I do so partly because I am myself a product of campus ministry. I owe it to campus ministry for being a committed Christian. Even more importantly, I owe it to campus ministry for eventually becoming a priest in the Anglican Church. I accepted the Lord Jesus Christ in my life after hearing the gospel from seminarians who visited and witnessed to us at Kangema High School in Murang'a, Kenya, in January 1970. It was a boarding high school. Looking back, this marked the beginning of my Church ministry as a lay minister and, eventually, as an ordained priest.

As God would have it, I returned to Kangema High School as a teacher where I taught for five years. I was soon appointed patron of the Christian Union. This non-stipendiary position enabled me to work with the students, organizing them for Sunday services, inviting the local Anglican minister to come and celebrate Holy Communion, inviting speakers for Sunday services, and organizing students for weekend challenges and youth camps during the holidays. I thoroughly enjoyed these extra-curriculum responsibilities. Soon, I realized that I was the *de facto* school chaplain for my high school.

Through this tent-making ministry, I gradually realized that God had all along been calling me to the ordained ministry. I went through the normal interviews with the bishop's examining chaplains. I was given the green light to go to seminary. In December, 1977, I resigned my teaching job, and on January 3, 1978, I entered St. Paul's United Theological Seminary, Limuru, Kenya, in preparation for ordained ministry. I graduated in 1980 and was ordained deacon in the same year and as priest in 1981.

As far as I know, there is no theological school strictly set apart for training college chaplains. College chaplains go through the regular seminaries to train as parish priests. In the process, some of these seminarians realize that God is calling them to a ministry with young adults. Others may have realized this call to youth ministry long before they entered seminary. After going through the normal courses for seminary training, such persons go out and start working with young adults, some of them as college chaplains.

Like many other seminarians, I went to seminary to train as a parish priest. Since my ordination, I have served the Church in a variety of capacities, as parish priest, seminary principal or dean, associate rector and priest in charge. But none of these ministries has been as fulfilling as working with young adults particularly as college chaplain and director of college ministry. I look back and see people who helped me as a young adult, people who believed and saw potential in me, and people who nurtured and encouraged me. I seek to do so for the young adults that God brings into my life. College ministry is a ministry of encouragement. This is true both for the chaplain and for the students alike. I am prone to say to my colleagues that college ministry cannot be done by one who allows him or herself to be discouraged. The college chaplain must be encouraged to encourage. I am honored and privileged to have done this ministry on a full-time basis for more than ten years.

Throughout these years of college ministry, I have encountered many new campus ministers. Some of these are newly appointed by their bishops or called by College Ministry Boards to do this ministry. Some of them are newly ordained deacons or priests from seminary who find themselves thrust into campus ministry. Many of these new campus ministers have found themselves at a loss as to where to begin. Although I have been working with college students in one way or other throughout my nearly thirty years of ordained ministry, I certainly groped and yearned for the kind of help provided in this book. College ministry has many pitfalls. Dodging them is essential to a fulfilling college ministry.

As it becomes evident in this book, I cannot claim I was successful in the art of dodging these pitfalls. I, therefore, offer this book for all new campus ministers called to do this most important ministry. I truly hope that this book comes in handy to them in wedging their way through their particular pitfalls. I also offer this book to all young adults striving to seek God in their lives.

The Rev. Dr. Samson N. Gitau

May the guiding light lead them to enlightenment and enable them to own their faith in God.

I also offer this book to the Church. More often than not, college ministry is treated as a side ministry that will be funded after every other ministry has been funded. By the same token, college ministry is often the most vulnerable. It's often the first to be cut if and when diocesan finances become uncertain. My experience shows that even those who would be expected to advocate for college ministry such as bishops, will not hesitate to cut college ministry if the funding of their own positions are threatened. This has been my experience as the pages of this book will show. I, therefore, offer this book to Church leaders, bishops, and diocesan committees who are often faced with the choice to either keep or cut college ministry. To this leadership, I categorically say that cutting the ministry with young adults is not and should never be an option if we care for the future of the church.

Reflecting on this ministry, I see that I am truly blessed to have had the opportunity to serve as the Director of College Ministry in the Diocese of West Tennessee for ten years. Today, October 1, 2007, I begin my terminal sabbatical leave. By the time I am through with my sabbatical, I will have served in this capacity for ten years. Ten years is a reasonably long time for a person to be in one assignment. So far, this is the longest ministry I have done in my 27 years of ordained ministry. For this, I will ever be grateful. I have always wanted to write on college ministry. I have, therefore decided to spend most of my sabbatical leave writing my memoirs on this ministry that I have dedicated myself to these ten years.

In 1998, I was associate rector of St. James's Episcopal Church, Cambridge, Massachusetts, when I learned that my rector, Christopher Leighton, was about to take a new assignment. As my wife and I prayed about this situation and weighed the options before us, I reduced my options to either allow myself to be appointed interim rector for a period of one and may be a maximum of two years and then face the reality of looking for another assignment, or start looking for a new assignment at that time. The second option made more sense. I, therefore, placed my name with the Church Deployment Office at *815* in New York where my credentials were matched with those of the search committee in the Diocese of West Tennessee. The search committee of West Tennessee was looking for a college chaplain to serve colleges in the Memphis area. As I came to understand later, the committee had already gone through an unsuccessful search. This was their second attempt to find a person for this job.

The committee invited me for an interview with them. Neither I, nor my wife, had ever been down South. The idea of going South from New England sounded novel and even crazy to me and my friends in Cambridge. Some of my friends said as much, wondering why anybody from Boston would consider going down South. But I decided that I had nothing to lose in giving it a shot. I reasoned that since the search committee was paying for my round trip ticket to and from Memphis, it wouldn't hurt to go down and interview with them.

One of my friends, indeed the only friend I had known from Memphis and now living in Boston, impressed me with the South and its low cost of living. However, now that I have been here these many years, I cannot say that this is necessarily true. My friend recommended that I read *"At the River I Stand,"* by Joan T. Beifuss which I did. I started looking up stuff about the South and its history. I discovered the centrality of Memphis to the civil rights movement. The more I read about the South, the more interested I became and the more convinced I became that I needed to come for the interview with the search committee. My first interview went well and some of my fears were alleviated as I realized that Memphians were ordinary people like the Bostonians with whom I was familiar. I was invited for my second interview and basically offered the job of college chaplain.

My job description was to start programs in four colleges in Memphis - University of Memphis, Rhodes College, LeMoyne-Owen College and Christian Brothers University. The task was daunting, but I was determined to do it. Lilian had come with me on this second interview. A realtor recommended by the search committee showed us a number of properties. We wanted to get a home as close to the four colleges as possible. We finally saw a house in Midtown and Lilian fell in love with it. The search was over. We made an offer which was accepted and we were on our way to Memphis. We have been in this house ever since.

Writing to Bishop Coleman, then Bishop of the Diocese of West Tennessee, I told him that I felt like Abraham in the Hebrew Bible called to leave his homeland of Haran and all his kindred and move down south. Abraham had trusted God and did what God asked him to do. He was never disappointed. Indeed Abraham's act of obedience to God was reckoned to him as righteousness. There is no doubt that Abraham was most apprehensive in undertaking the journey to go down south. I again reasoned that all I needed was to trust God and what He was calling me to do.

When I informed my friends, especially at St. James's Episcopal Church, that we were moving down South, most of them thought that I was crazy to do such a thing. But I had no doubt that God had called me to do college ministry, working with young adults in equipping them in their spiritual journeys and struggles in life. In reality, the move from Boston to Memphis was not all that hard. I rationalized that going down South could not be crazier than coming from Kenya to the US. If I had survived a major eastward move of over 8,000 miles from Kenya to the United States of America, surely, this couldn't be worse than that. I was already used to cultural shocks and accents. Above all, I wanted to be faithful in doing God's will, to go where God wanted me to go.

I had had prior background working with college students. In 1984 - 1989 I was the principal of McGregor Bible College in Kenya, training seminarians in their preparation for ordained ministry. In 1990-1991, I was the interim Episcopal college chaplain at Boston University filling in for Father Jep Streit, gone on sabbatical leave. But this was the first time that I was called to focus my energy on working with young adults in college ministry. My love for young adults motivated me to assume the daunting task of serving multi-campuses in college ministry in the Diocese of West Tennessee.

Prior to my coming to the Episcopal Diocese of West Tennessee, there was no active college ministry

The Rev. Dr. Samson N. Gitau

in any of the four colleges I had been invited to serve. Certainly there never had been any Episcopal presence at LeMoyne-Owen and Christian Brothers University. Attempts had been made to reach out to Rhodes College from Grace/St. Luke's Church. This had not been successful and lacked the much needed continuity. At Barth House, serving the University of Memphis, there had been an on and off presence and occasionally a full-time college chaplain. The last full-time chaplain prior to my coming was the late Dr. Robert Watson.

College ministry at Barth House dates back to 1926, when the University of Memphis used to be known as Normal School and later Memphis Teacher Training College. The faculty then saw the need to provide spiritual nourishment to their students beyond their academic training. St. John's Episcopal Church also got involved in this ministry with the Church Women providing food to the students. A residential property was eventually bought and the first worship services were held in the garage of that house.

The current Barth House building which includes, a chapel and a multi-purpose room, two offices, a kitchen and sacristy, was built in 1967. Bishop Barth, then Bishop of Tennessee, was instrumental in establishing the Barth House property, rightly named after him. The chapel was named St. Theodore's Chapel. Barth House has been a haven for many students with some of them meeting and establishing lasting relationships, sometimes leading to marriage. But by the time I came to the Diocese of West Tennessee in August 1998, Barth House had been converted to a Diocesan resource center with books, videos, and other literature, checked out and used for

Christian education by members of the local parishes. Mrs. Elise Williams faithfully dispensed these resources to those who needed them. Sometimes, a visiting clergy supplied on Wednesdays where a handful of students gathered for Holy Eucharist. An Episcopal presence was clearly lacking at the University of Memphis.

Right from the outset, I was determined to establish a vibrant and diverse college chaplaincy particularly at Barth House, in addition to establishing programs in the other three campuses. The commuter nature of the University of Memphis necessitated a variety of programs so that if a student could not make it to one of them he/she could come to the other. I maintained a midweek service on Wednesdays. The home-cooked lunch by Ms. Williams made it even more attractive to the students. Soon I established a group of faithful students who regularly attended this service. I also started Morning Prayer. Morning Prayer is not the most popular service for students especially when it is at 8:00 A.M. Most students are either still asleep or sleepily heading to class. But for my own spiritual nurture and opportunity to pray for students, faculty and staff, I established this service. At its best, there might be anywhere to ten participants. At its worst, which was frequent, there were two of us doing Morning Prayer. I have come to enjoy this discipline of reading the daily office.

I started a Sunday evening service at 6:00 P.M. This became our main worship service followed by a home-cooked dinner and fellowship. The fellowship gave the students and me the chance to discuss issues ranging from what I had said in my homily, to what was currently going on at the campus, at church, with the country or the society in general. The diverse nature of the participants of this service made it the most enjoyable and productive of our college ministry programs.

But before I get ahead of myself by delving into college ministry programming and its impact on college students and campus community in general, I need to address the questions: "Why do college ministry?" "What is our biblical mandate for doing college ministry?" "Why should the church be concerned with college students and their spiritual welfare?" The next chapter will be geared to addressing these pertinent questions.

Chapter Two

Biblical Foundations for Ministry with Young Adults

"I am writing to you young men (read, "young adults"), because you are strong, and the word of God abides in you, and you have overcome the evil one." (1 John 2:14)

John the elder must have had a lot of faith in young adults, so much faith in the youth as to take the time to write to them commending them for their gifts endowed upon them by God. First, most young adults are strong. Young adults have much energy, but not just physical energy. Young adults are more innovative. More entrepreneurial. More into risk taking. Whereas this last quality may be viewed as a liability, the adage is true "no risk no gain." One major hindrance in the Church today is that we are often stuck with antiquated ways of doing things that do not work, but we simply will not try any other way. The mantra is, "This is how things have always been done and we are going to continue doing them that way." It was Einstein who said, "It is madness to continue doing things the same way and expect different results." If we expect different and better results, we must take the risk of varying our methods. Young adults are a great resource in this process. We must engage them in church government and planning if ever we expect to break away from the *status quo*. On the other hand, if we are contented with the *status quo*, let's continue keeping young adults at bay.

Stereotypes

John the elder continues to commend young adults for allowing the word of God to abide in them. Well, that too goes contrary to popular thinking. The general mind set is to degrade young adults and to lay every vice of our society squarely at their feet. Young adults can and do have a strong faith that needs to be fanned to brilliantly burn. On the other hand, it is psychologically true that if a parent persistently scolds his her/her child and calls him/her stupid and good for nothing, the negative image is gradually reinforced in the child's life. The opposite is true. Affirm the good in the young person and he/she will go ahead and live that affirmation. Could it be true that the church is consciously or unconsciously affirming negative attitudes and stereotypes in our young adults? Could it be true that we are advertently or inadvertently sending the wrong signal to our young adults? John has a different norm. Affirm the positive in our young adults for a stronger and healthier Church.

"You have overcome the evil one." Really? The society, the Church included, tends to see young adults as already overcome by the evil one. It is as if everybody else in society is perfect except young adults! The society tends to blame young adults for everything that is wrong in society. This may be through simple statements as "I do not know what has become of this generation." Implication? Things have gone wrong and who is to blame? Young adults, of course! But John sees it differently. Young adults can and have overcome the world. It's all a question of attitude. It is a question of which wolf we are feeding with our words and actions - the wolf of defeat or the wolf of victory in our young adults.

There is no better place to nurture and positively affirm our young adults for who they are and who they can become, than in college ministry. College ministry is the new frontier for evangelism. College ministry is the new frontier for building a strong Church. College ministry is the new frontier for building a strong generation. The sooner the Church wakes up to this reality, the better. But what exactly are the reasons for doing college ministry? Why should the church be concerned at all with college students?

Why Do Campus Ministry?

This is a pertinent question not only because campus ministry is neither an income generating ministry, nor a ministry that, in most cases, is able to be self-sustaining. Most campus ministries are almost wholly dependent on the diocesan annual budgets or some endowment made in the past. So let's face it, campus ministry is a drain on the diocesan, or in some cases, parish budgets. In fact, campus ministry is so much perceived as a budgetary drain that whenever there is a financial crunch in the church budgeting, campus ministry is sure to be the first line item to be placed on the chopping board. Off it goes!

Distinguishing the Urgent from the Important

Chopping college ministry programs was the norm in the Episcopal Church in the 1960s and 70s. Dioceses across the board cut campus ministries. There was a financial crunch, not unlike what we have been going through in this country. Parish and diocesan budgets were not balancing. Some programs had to go. You guessed it! Campus ministry was in the forefront of those line items placed on the chopping board. This was easy to do. Campus ministry was not and is not an income generating ministry. The Church had other more urgent ministries to do. Campus ministry was not one of them. But as one of my wise bishop friends was prone to say, "We must learn to distinguish between what is urgent and what is important." Unfortunately, most people and even institutions are inclined to pursue what is urgent and neglect what is important. The church is guilty of this offense in its dealing with young adults, in general, and college ministry in particular.

Irreparable Damage

The results from these misinformed and ill-thought Church decisions were immediate and detrimental. The number of young adults dropped from the Church. An obvious shortage of young clergy ensured. This problem has persisted to the present day, thanks to decisions made in the sixties and seventies. The number of young clergy, that is, clergy under the age of thirty-five years is negligible in the Episcopal Church in particular. This small number is most revealing of the irreparable damage done to the church in its decision to cut campus ministry budgets. As a person who has served in Commission on Ministry (COM) for more than six years, I have found that almost every candidate that came before us discerning for ordained ministry did so either as a second or third career or even more. One cannot help wondering whether God deliberately skips calling young and fresh persons and settles for tired and worn out second and third career persons. One cannot help wondering whether God is interested in young adults just as much as he interested in older people. When the church persistently recruits and admits old people to seminary, eventually the young adults get the message. Ordained ministry is not for us. We can be anything else we want, but not ministers in the church. We have to wait until we are fifty or sixty to even start thinking about it.

Seed for Future Harvest

To ask the question "Why do campus ministry?" is like asking "Why plant the seed while one can eat it?" This is a hard choice in agrarian societies which constantly rely on rain for their crops. Oftentimes drought comes followed by famine. The farmer is always hard pressed to either cook and eat the precious seed or persevere and preserve it against all difficulties for planting when the rains finally come. The foolish farmer easily chooses to eat the seed and solve the immediate problem, but the wise farmer preserves the seed against all difficulties and temptations to cook and eat it. The wise farmer well knows that soon or later the rains will come and he/she will need the seed to plant in order to overcome the famine. Sure enough, eventually the rains come and the wise farmer plants his/her seed and looks forward to a harvest. The foolish farmer has no seed to plant and often resorts to begging for survival. The Psalmist succinctly puts it this way "Those who go out weeping, carrying the seed, will come again with joy shouldering their sheaves of their harvest." (Ps. 126:7). The opposite is also true; those who in their short sightedness eat the seed will sadly come to an empty home with nothing to eat.

It is prudent to heed the wise advice of the sage author of Ecclesiastes to "Cast your bread upon the waters, for you will find it after many days" (Eccl. 11:1). In the same vein, this author points out: "He who observes the wind will not sow" (11:4). There are many reasons why the Church could be tempted to eat the seed of college ministry, but the Church must resist the temptation to do so. There are many reasons why the Church would be tempted to keep its bread rather than to liberally sow it, but the Church must not give in to such temptations. There are many reasons why the church could be tempted to observe the wind as an excuse not to plant. But the church must not give in to this temptation. To do so would be like a parent to argue that it is a very hard job to invest in raising children. After all, children are a drain to resources. They are a bad investment. Who said that raising children is an easy job? Who said it is a good investment? However, any sensible person will know that to give in to such an argument, no matter how persuasive, is to cripple society. Unfortunately, in chopping college ministry budgets, the church is doing exactly that - crippling the Church. The Church cannot have its cake and eat it at the same time!

Parable on Two Foundations

Jesus' parable on the two foundations is equally relevant for us today (Matthew 7:24-27; Luke 7:46-49). There was a man who wanted to build himself a house. However, he was not wise enough to consult an architect on what was needed to build a durable house. He was not wise enough to dig and lay a deep and strong foundation. He was not wise enough to use well-mixed concrete and supporting steel bars for his foundation. He was a man in a hurry. He was a man prone to dealing with the urgent at the expense of the important. All he wanted was to build himself a house. How that house turned out was the least of his concerns. And sure enough, the man built himself a house. Unfortunately, he built it upon the sand. Gradually the rains fell and the floods came and the winds blew and beat upon the house. And yes, you guessed it! Down came the house tumbling down! Jesus concludes: "and great was the fall of the house."

This is a metaphor for a Church that talks about growth and survival without investing its time and resources in its young adults. The rains and floods and winds of life will surely come. They will surely beat upon the house of the Church. It will certainly come tumbling down. I know only too well that these days most Christians are not keen on hearing prophecies of doom. To be sure, one only needs to ask such Old Testament prophets like Amos. The people hated with passion these type of prophets and their prophecies. Prophecies of judgment tend to rub us the wrong way, making us uncomfortable. We would rather have the message of complacency that puts us to a slumber. But prophecy against poorly built houses is right before our eyes. "Great will be the fall of that church."

House on the Rock

But an authentic prophet also knows that it doesn't have to be that way. There is always an exit from disaster if we care to listen and heed the warning. So there was another builder in Jesus' parable of the foundations. This was the wise person. This man well knew that for him to have a durable house, he needed a strong foundation. So he chose to build upon the rock. There is no doubt that this second builder consulted all the relevant experts. He no doubt calculated the cost and the time it would take to build himself a durable house. In the end, this builder realized that the cost and the time spent were worth it. Eventually, the man finished his house. It was built on solid rock for its foundation. And sure enough, the rains eventually fell. The floods came and the winds blew. These forces combined to beat upon the house. The house stood its ground. The man had built

Pitfalls

himself a durable house. It was worth it. This, too, is a metaphor of the Church. The Church that seeks to build itself upon the foundation of a well-nurtured young adult population is wise. The efforts are worth it. This Church will certainly survive and continue to grow strong when the rains, the floods and winds of life beat upon it. These forces will be unable to overwhelm the Church. They simply cannot.

Hard economic times are not the time to eat the planting seed. They are the appropriate times to persevere and invest wisely. Financial crises are sure to come. But these crises only come and go. So for the Church to cut young adult programs to solve financial problems is to be foolish and short-sighted. A good friend of mine put it more succinctly, "it is like burning the pews to heat the church." There is no doubt that there are many ways for trouble-shooting the problem. But as Stephen White rightly points out "Any approach to fund campus ministries other than through restricted endowments of sufficient size to fund a full-time chaplain and a meaningful program merely gives lip service to campus ministry and willfully neglects the future vitality of our church." (*College Chaplain*, p. 19). The church must walk the walk and boldly put its action where its mouth is. Church ministry to young adults is either crucial to church growth and health or it is not. If it is, there will always be ways and means of funding this ministry as long as there is a Church. There certainly are and will always be men and women of good will in the Church who are acutely aware of the importance of investing in our young adults. These men and women of good will no doubt will sacrificially give to preserve the seed of the

Church. The Church leadership must pave the way to this need and solution.

Campus ministry is an investment for and by the church. Failure to do it is like a worker who decides to spend all his/her earning and makes no saving, no pension saving at all. Come retirement, the person will have nothing to fall back to. I recall a priest under whom I served as a transitional deacon. He had the option of sending part of his salary to the provident fund for his retirement or to spend it. He chose the latter option. His argument was: "Let me use it now that I have it." Come retirement, this priest received a very small pension check. He had himself to blame. A Church that fails to take seriously the ministry of its young adults has itself to blame for its gradual and eventual demise. This church risks recycling itself to extinction.

Campus ministry is a forum for providing the right atmosphere for young adults to hear God's voice at the right time. Let's face it. If we lose our young adults while they are in college, we will be lucky to get them again when they are raising families if ever we get them at all. On the other hand, if we get them when they come to college, chances are we will keep them for life. Put in another way, if we cannot afford to invest in our young adults when they desperately need us, let's stop decrying the paucity of young adults in the Church. Let us not expect that when these young adults graduate they will readily support the Church with their resources.

College life has many demands. There are many callings in addition to the academic pursuit. There are fraternities and sororities. There are all kinds of sports, some of which can be very demanding. There is much freedom too. For the first time the young adult has left the nest. He/she is suddenly free from parental tethers. He/she is free to make personal decisions of every kind. For most of them, there are friends to make too. Some can be helpful friends, others are toxic friends. They are the kind of friends that easily draw the young adult into the misuse of their newly found freedom. This newly found freedom can be expended in weekend parties, hangout joints, among others. Campus ministry provides an alternative to most of these callings and forces. Campus ministry provides a forum where the worn out and sometimes confused young adults can come for consolation, assurance and guidance. Campus ministry provides a home away from home.

College can be a very lonely experience for some young adults. This is particularly so in the first year of college. For these students, campus ministry provides a home away from home. It provides a caring community that allows young adults to own and practice their faith. Up to this time, most young adults have professed a 'parental faith.' Most of them have gone to church because their parents said to. They have done so because they wish to please their parents. In college, the young adults are challenged to own their faith. This is a crucially important period in the faith development of young adults. If they seek and own their faith at this time, chances are they will keep it for life. On the other hand, if they lose their faith, chances are they will lose it for life. Campus ministry provides continuity, and to some extent, discontinuity between the practice of 'parental faith' and personal faith, between the EYC faith and activities and college-professed young adult personal faith. The Church has a mandate to cater to its young adults. Scriptures are full of examples of men and women who are called by God in their youth. A few examples from the Bible will suffice in demonstrating the case for biblical foundations of ministry with young adults.

Samuel

Samuel was the son of Elkanah and Hannah, Elkanah's supposedly barren second wife. Therefore, when Samuel was born, he was a most precious gift from God to Hannah, his mother, the never relenting petitioner to God in her quest for a child of her own. God heard Hannah's prayers. He blessed her with a baby boy. Hannah was ecstatic with joy for her most precious gift from God. As an expression of her heartfelt gratitude, Hannah gave the gift right back to God. As soon as Samuel was weaned from his nursing, Hannah donated him back to God for the temple ministry in Shiloh, under the instruction of Eli the priest.

Hannah must have realized that God had a wonderful plan for her son. She must have realized that for that plan to be realized, Samuel must be placed in the right place. To pursue the seed metaphor a bit further, in surrendering her son to the temple, Hannah was planting her seed for future growth. She was doing so with many tears of self-denial and sacrifice yet, ever grateful that she now had something she could give back to God. Which mother does not want to spend quality time with her child? Which presumed barren woman, when she finally conceives, will readily give up her child for another to raise? But Hannah was doing so with the mixed joy of hope. Her faith in the God who had answered her prayers persuaded her to believe that only by surrendering her most precious gift from God would God eventually perfect the miracle of his birth. Unknown to Hannah, her gift to God was the conduit through which God would again revive the hitherto dormant prophetic voice in Israel. She was right. The seed she sowed in that decision never disappointed her. Samuel went on to become the greatest and last judge over Israel. He went on to become the greatest priest that ancient Israel had ever known. Samuel was the king maker, anointing Saul and David, as the first and second kings of Israel respectively. Samuel presided over the transition between the amphictyony and the monarchy. It is no wonder, therefore, that Samuel went on to become one of the most influential men of God that ancient Israel had ever known. There is no doubt that the secret behind this great success was his mother, Hannah, who well realized that in order to hear God, one must be in the right place at the right time.

God called Samuel from his youth. I suggest that this was only possible because Samuel was at the right place at the right time. He was in the temple in the company of Eli the priest. The temple was Samuel's home. The temple ministry was his preoccupation. When finally called, even though at first he was unsure about who was calling him, the more experienced priest, Eli, was on hand to guide and direct Samuel in his discernment. That is precisely the role of campus ministry. It is to provide a forum of nurture and guidance for our young adults.

It's no wonder that many people go through life without ever hearing and discerning God's plan in their lives. Primary reason? They are not in the right place at the right time. They are not attuned to the ever broadcasting God. Hannah and Samuel present an example for us. When finally called, the well-coached Samuel was able to say: "Master, speak, for thy servant hears" (1 Sam. 3:10). If we want young adults to hear God's voice, we must place them where they are more prone to hear that voice. We must facilitate the encounter between God and our young adults. Samuel took over from Eli as priest in God's house. There is no doubt that Samuel was well trained and prepared for the ministry that lay ahead of him. Hannah and Eli were persons of insight that made this training and preparation possible. The scripture is right on target when it points out that "where there is no vision, people perish." This is true both for the church, the nation or any other institution for that matter. The church must not be left behind in casting a vision for its future leadership.

Jeremiah

I was recently invited by one of my parishioners to talk to her troubled class of teenagers. I shared with them the vision that motivated me in life in growing up in a rural village in Kenya, eventually becoming an Anglican priest. In an attempt to encourage them, I asked these teenagers to tell me what their dreams and visions were in life. Each one of them took a turn to say who they wanted to become. What one of these young adults said still stands out in my mind. He said: "When I grow up, I want to be an NFL player." That took me by surprise. Had the young man said he wanted to be a doctor, or teacher or lawyer, or any of the other traditional professions, as most of the others had said, I would have understood it. But it was hard for me to reconcile in my mind a young man picking NFL as a career. I never heard any college that taught NFL or any other sport as a major. Each athlete I have encountered has a professional major in college. Sport is like a minor, even though many of them end up in making a career in sports. I must confess that as a non-sports person, my thinking was biased. I must admit that as a person who grew up knowing that academia is the way to success, I was one-sided in my judgment. But there again is my point. We are likely to promote and pursue what we know and believe.

My experience with the young man has a bearing with what is happening in the Church and its relationship with young adults. Could it be that it is not the kids who do not want to aspire to these offices, but that we as the Church and society do not encourage them to do so? Could it be that the Church is biased against young adults aspiring to Church ministry as ordained ministers? Could it be that when one of our young adults declares that he/she wants to be an ordained minister we, are surprised with what we hear? Could it be that we could and may be have implicitly or explicitly done what we could to discourage young adults from choosing ordained ministry as a vocation? It is evident that we easily accept young adults picking business administration, social work, teaching, medicine, law, among others careers, but would be thoroughly surprised if such kids suddenly said, "I want to be a priest or a bishop." The truth is that we do not expect God to call them to these offices when they are in college but if at all, later in life, as a second or third career. Do we truly believe that God calls both the young and old alike?

Jeremiah is a classic example of a young adult called by God for God's ministry. To be sure, Jeremiah did not wake up one day and declare that he wanted to be God's prophet to the people of Israel. Oh No! Nobody wanted to be called to this job, let alone aspire to it. Here is Jeremiah's call by God.

Now the word of the Lord came to me saying
Before I formed you in the womb I knew you,
and before you were born I consecrated you;
I appointed you a prophet to the nations.
Then I said: Ah, Lord God! Behold, I do not know how to speak,
for I am only a youth.
But the Lord said to me.
"Do not say, "I am only a youth;
for to all whom I send you, you shall go
and whatever I command you, you shall speak.
Be not afraid of them,
for I am with you to deliver you," says the Lord
Then the Lord put forth his hand
and touched my mouth;
and the Lord said to me,
"Behold, I have put my words in your mouth.
See, I have set you this day over nations and over kingdoms,
to pluck up and break down,

to destroy and overthrow
To build and to plant" (Jer. 1:4-10).

Like Samuel, Jeremiah, was in the right place at the right time for God to call him. Jeremiah came from a Levitical heritage (see Deut. 18:13-20). He was called to be a prophet like Moses. He was called to be Yahweh's messenger. This is well articulated in the prophet's call. God touches his mouth with the words:

"Then the Lord put forth his hand
and touched my mouth;
and the Lord said to me,
"Behold, I have put my words in your mouth."

From then on Jeremiah was God's spokesperson. He spoke on behalf of God. When he spoke to God's people, his words were: "Thus says, YHWH." They were no longer Jeremiah's words, but God's own words.

It is evident that God had a wonderful plan for Jeremiah and consequently, for all young people. God has a purpose for the life of every young adult out there. To Jeremiah he says "Before I formed you in the womb I knew you, and before you were born I consecrated you." Later on, YHWH reminds Jeremiah regarding this special plan for him. He says: For I have a plan for you, a plan for good and not for evil" (Jer. 29:11). Many persons, including young adults, go through life without the realization that life has both meaning and purpose. The church has a divine mandate to ensure that God's people are available to be used by God when he calls them. God's plan and discernment cannot be realized in a vacuum. They are realized in Church forums. To deny young adults a place in this Church is to deny them God's call.

John Mark

The story of John Mark is one of the most compelling stories illustrating why the Church should take seriously its ministry with young adults. Mark was an eyewitness when Jesus instituted the Last Supper, popularly known as the Holy Eucharist. It is the primary focus of worship for most main line churches today. Tradition has it that Jesus celebrated this sacrament in the home of John Mark's mother. It's always curious why Mark's father is not mentioned. May be Mark's mother was a rich widow. Whatever the case was, Mark was present when Jesus instituted this great sacrament with his twelve disciples. Mark most possibly served as an acolyte or a page in this most holy celebration. What he saw, heard and witnessed impacted the rest of his life.

Mark was an eyewitness in the trials and persecutions of Jesus before the Sanhedrin. He was an eyewitness, not only to these most sobering happenings, but also to how all the disciples, the closest friends of Jesus, abandoned him when he needed them most. To be sure, Mark, himself, was not an angel. In his passion narrative, Mark describes an aspect in these events that only an eyewitness could have recorded. He pointed out that when push came to shove, and it became evident that association with Jesus meant death for any person who ventured to do so, a young man ran away for his dear life. The situation was so dire that the young man, most probably, John Mark himself, threw away his covering cloak and ran away naked. This was not a heroic thing to do for any person but Mark nevertheless recorded it, no doubt, to show that only by the grace of God were he and others redeemed.

Mark had two other crucial associations that enabled him to become a most effective witness of the Lord Jesus Christ and the Gospel. Extra-biblical accounts show that Mark was closely associated with Peter. Other accounts such as from John the Elder, point out that Mark was Peter's interpreter in his preaching ministry. It is most probable that Peter preached in Aramaic and that the young and more learned John Mark interpreted the sermons in Greek, the lingua franca of the day. This close association with Peter enabled Mark to gather very helpful reminiscences as a first-hand eye witness of the Lord Jesus Christ. When Peter finally died in Rome, Mark compiled the materials he had acquired in order to write the first gospel on the life and teaching of Jesus around A.D. 65.

Mark's second association was with Paul. Mark was one of those few people who accompanied Paul and Barnabas in their first missionary journey. Mark was a nephew of Barnabas, a familial connection that may have earned him a place in this first missionary journey. But even more compelling was the impact of the good news Mark had heard from Jesus, his death, his resurrection and his commission to his disciples. The impact of these events upon the young man was so compelling that Mark was ready to venture on a missionary journey to go and tell others about Jesus. Young adults are most adventurous and eager to share their testimonies.

The missionary journey went well, that is, until the team reached Pamphylia, on the shores of Asia Minor, modern day Turkey. At this point, the journey became too much for John Mark. Scholars suggest that the team was attacked by mosquitoes that made their lives miserable. Mark couldn't take it any more. He quit the rest of the mission trip and took the next ship back home. Paul and Barnabas continued with the mission trip and in spite of hardships, planted churches in Lystra, Derbe and Iconium, all in Asia Minor. Satisfied with the mission, the team went back home to Jerusalem.

When it was time to go out on the second missionary journey, Mark declared his intention to join the team again. Paul couldn't have any of that. He declared that he was not going to take a quitter with him. It appears that Paul here represents the traditional stereotype of the Church. Young adults are quitters. You simply cannot trust them. You are better off leaving them out. It's a bad idea to invest in young adults. It's a waste of time and resources.

But Barnabas had a different idea. True to his name, son of encouragement, Barnabas had seen in Mark something that gave him hope. He saw in Mark the future and vitality of the Church. Barnabas was a man of great insight. He argued that they should give Mark a second chance. Paul stuck to his guns and totally refused to barge his ground. The team divided. Paul took Silas and they went on the second missionary journey. Barnabas took Mark and went to Cyprus.

By every count, Paul and Silas did a great job. They planted more churches across Asia. They revived and encouraged those churches they had already planted. Unfortunately we do not hear very much about Barnabas and Mark and their accomplishments in Cyprus. But whereas the record may be silent on what actually happened in Cyprus, the rest of the story has a great ending. As already pointed out, Mark went on to write the first gospel ever written on the life and teaching of Jesus. Mark preserved for us and for posterity to come, the greatest treasure of the Church. In so doing, Mark set an example to Matthew and Luke who both used his gospel as a rich resource to write their own gospel accounts. There is no doubt that even John was influenced by Mark in writing the fourth gospel, if not in substance, in motivation and spirit.

Were it not for the likes of John Mark's mother who no doubt raised him with the word of God, how else could we have had the great wealth we have today? Were it not for the likes of Peter and Barnabas who embraced and nurtured the talents they saw in Mark, how else could we have had this great wealth on the gospel of the life and teaching of Jesus Christ? Were it not for the likes of Barnabas who gave Mark a second chance and who generously invested in him when all evidence indicated that it was better to do otherwise, the church would be much poorer. Barnabas represents the visionary Church. Barnabas clearly realized that where there is no vision, the church would perish. His vision saved the Church.

Timothy

The Greek name Timothy *(Timotheus)* means "one who honors God." The Timothy of the New Testament was a young man, a trusted and faithful companion of Paul. Paul had discovered Timothy in Asia Minor (Acts 16:1-3), where he had already established himself in the Galatian Churches - Derbe, Lystra and Iconium, as a dedicated servant of the gospel of the Lord Jesus Christ. Timothy was well spoken of by the Christians in these churches. As we have already seen Paul had lost the services of John Mark, the young man who had accompanied him and Barnabas in their missionary journey. He was most eager to get a replacement. He therefore enlisted Timothy, another young man to join him and Silas in their second missionary journey. Timothy was eager to venture out for God.

Timothy immediately established himself as a trusted and faithful companion of Paul and Silas. The trio signed the First and Second letters to the Thessalonians. This trio had planted the church in Thessalonica, a seaport of commerce and later capital of the Macedonia Province. Soon after, the trio left Thessalonica and went to Athens. In Athens, Paul agonized on the fate of his converts in Thessalonica and for the young church they had planted there. For one, Paul knew that these young Christians were suffering persecution from their fellow Thessalonians for abandoning the worship of their local deities like Dionysus, the god of fertility. Paul also agonized for Christians in Thessalonica because members of this young Church needed to be better established in the faith.

Unable to bear the anxiety any longer, Paul sent Timothy back to Thessalonica to find out the welfare of the Thessalonian Christians and to establish them in the faith (1 Tim. 3:1-5). Timothy visited with the Thessalonians and returned with a glowing report regarding the growing faith, love and steadfastness of the Thessalonian

Christians. The report was most encouraging to Paul and Silas.

In sending Timothy out on an important mission to the Thessalonians, Paul was showing his full trust of the young adult. Paul did not stop to argue that the youth belong to the church of tomorrow. He did not wait for Timothy to "grow up" in order to entrust him with an important responsibility. Timothy, the young adult was part and parcel of the Church. He did not have to wait to serve this church in the future. He was its minister at that time. The Church would be well advised to take cue from Paul's example in his dealings with Timothy. First, we must learn from past mistakes of leaving out young adults and move on in the right direction. Second, we do not have to wait until eternity to recruit and employ young adults in Church ministry. Now is the time to put young adult representatives in vestries, diocesan conventions, General Convention and in other church committees and organizations. Now is the time to show young adults that they are an integral part of the church today.

It is evident that in enlisting the help of Timothy, Paul already missed the services of John Mark. Could it be that Paul already regretted how he had dismissed Mark? Either, way, Paul seems to have learned from his mistake. He coveted the services of Timothy in Church ministry. He exhorted and encouraged Timothy in this ministry. Timothy was Paul's faithful companion and emissary in Church ministry. Paul repeatedly and fondly refers to Timothy in his letters to the Churches that he had planted (1 Thess. 1:1; Phil. 1:1; Col. 1:1; Philemon 1:1).

Paul refers to Timothy as having been set aside for church ministry through prophetic utterance. According to Paul, it is evident that Timothy was not just some kid coming forward for some adventure. His was a prophetic calling for church ministry. One would think that the same God who called Timothy through prophetic ministry is still interested in young adults and that he is still actively calling young adults for church ministry today.

Exhorting and encouraging him for this ministry, Paul says to Timothy, "Let no one despise your youth, but set the believers an example in speech and conduct, in love, in faith, in purity" (1 Tim 4:12). Looking at these exhortations, these are the same kind of things that young adults are downgraded upon - inexperience, bad examples, unbecoming language and behavior, irrational love, lack of sound faith and purity. Yet Paul clearly points out that it is in these very things that Timothy, and by extension, all Christian young adults, should exemplify to the rest of the believers. Timothy was well grounded in his faith, learned and modeled for him by his mother Eunice, and his grandmother Lois. The two women had heeded the words of scripture to teach a child in the way he/she should go and he/she will never depart from that way even when he/she grows old (Pro. 22:6). Young adulthood is the appropriate time to mold the church we want. Lose this opportunity and severely cripple the church.

It is evident from the call and ministry of Timothy that God calls both young and old alike to his ministry. It is therefore not coincidental that Paul uses the two pastoral letters addressed to Timothy alongside that addressed to Titus, to address the all important questions on the qualifications of church office holders - bishops and presbyters and deacons. The primary criteria for holding these offices are not age, but godly conduct and faithfulness to the calling.

Chapter Three

Models of Campus Ministry

"Now there are varieties of gifts, but the same Spirit; and there are varieties of service, but the same Lord; and there are varieties of working, but it is the same God who inspires them in every one." (1 Cor. 12:4-6)

Each college has its own unique ethos. Some colleges are very much into academics. Others are into sports. Some colleges are commuter colleges. Others are residential. Yet others are a mix between commuter and residential. Attempts to reach out to students must take into account these different varieties and ethos unique to each college. In short, there are varieties of colleges and ministry models. A model that works in one situation may not necessarily be imported to work in another. The important question to ask is whether or not a model in use in a particular situation is working or not. This calls for regular evaluation to ensure that the model in place in a particular college setting is delivering the desired results.

The Rev. Dr. Samson N. Gitau

Free Standing Model

The free standing college ministry is one that is located in one particular college campus where the chaplain has an office and possibly a religious house where students regularly gather for programs. The free standing college ministry model is the most ideal situation for college ministry. The model allows the chaplain to dedicate his/her time to the student ministry in this particular college. The model gives the chaplain the time to concentrate on student programs geared to this particular setting. It also allows the chaplain to have the freedom and flexibility to experiment with a wide variety of programs that otherwise may not be possible in a shared space or in a situation where different campuses are competing for his/her time. Unfortunately, the free standing model is also the most costly to run. The remuneration of the college chaplain, programming, insurance and maintenance of the free standing college center requires reliable financial support. Some of these centers may be supported from an endowment established years ago for college ministry and administered by the Diocese. Most others have to rely on year to year financial support from the Diocesan budget. In times of financial hardships, this puts the free standing model on very unsure ground, as the chaplain may often not know if his/her ministry will be sufficiently funded at the beginning of any year.

Parish-Based Model

There are at least two types of parish-based college ministry models. Both operate from a parish setting. In the first case, the setting is an actual parish located within or in the proximity of the campus. In some cases, the history between the parish and the campus dates to many years ago. The campus may be an offshoot of the parish that years ago started an academic institution as part of its ministry. Ministry to this type of chaplaincy may be the direct role of the rector/chaplain. Sometimes the parish may have a joint service for faculty and staff and students. In other cases, the parish-based model sets aside one particular service for students. Some of the advantages of the parish-based model include stability, reliability in financial support as well as vitality. With the fluid college community where turnover takes place every four years, the participation of regular parishioners, faculty and staff gives this model much desired stability. However, this model may experience tension between the regular parishioners and the transient community. Careful balance must be maintained by the leadership to diffuse any tension that may arise from this mix.

The parish-based model often provides a stable financial support. So from the diocesan point of view, the parish-based model is more cost effective. It does not cost the diocese a whole lot, if anything, to reach out to the college community. However, the same balance will need to be maintained to avoid domination from the more regular community on the basis of "he who pays the piper calls the tune." The parish-based college ministry model provides much needed vitality to the congregation. The congregation is multi-generational. Sermons are usually academic and thought provoking. The chaplain can only take his/her sermons for granted at his/her own peril. Fellowship and coffee hour reflect the academic atmosphere of the congregation. This type of parish-based model of college ministry does not exist in the Diocese of West Tennessee. But where it exists, such as, in the dioceses of Alabama and Mississippi, it seems to work well.

Visiting Clergy Model

I will call the second type of parish-based college ministry "the visiting clergy model." In this model, the parish is also normally within the proximity of the campus. The parish rector and his/her staff decide to extend their pastoral responsibility to the college community. In other instances, the parish is delegated by the diocesan bishop to reach out to a neighboring campus. This may be through a newly ordained deacon sharing his/her ministry between the parish and campus ministry with half of the deacon's compensation coming directly from the diocese. For all practical purposes, this model relies on the services of the visiting clergy, who may or may not be available for regular services or emergences with students. His/her priorities are not in college ministry. College ministry is only an outreach of the visiting clergy's parish. This is the type of college ministry model that has been tried without success in the Diocese of West Tennessee. If it worked, this would be the most cost effective model for doing college ministry. But as one who has served as supply clergy for small congregations, I know only too well how much effort and time would be required for this type of model to produce the much needed growth. At best, it's a maintenance ministry. It is a non-committal and certainly half-hearted way of doing college ministry.

Multiple Campuses Model

The multiple campuses model is one where a college minister is entrusted with two or more campuses. Usually the college chaplain will have an office on one of the campuses and reaches out to the other campuses where he/she has regular programs. Thus, the college chaplain operates like the old Methodist circuit rider dividing his/her time between the campuses.

As the director of college ministry in the Diocese of West Tennessee, this was my kind of arrangement. I had an office at Barth House, located at the University of Memphis, complete with a chapel, kitchen and dining, and two offices. This setting was ideal for a freestanding campus ministry. But it was from this base that I reached out to Rhodes College, Christian Brothers University and LeMoyne-Owen College. I divided my time among these four campuses where I had regular Bible study and worship services on each one of them.

The multi-campus ministry tends to be a combination of two or more models all blended together. In my particular case, the authorities in each of the other three campuses, usually the office of student affairs, provided me with a worshiping space where I regularly met with my students. At Rhodes College, for instance, Bellingrath Chapel and the adjoining meeting room were ideal for my ministry there. We would gather in the chapel for worship and in the meeting room for refreshments and conversation. At Christian Brothers and LeMoyne-Owen, a meeting room was provided for Bible study and fellowship thereafter. At CBU, St. Joseph's chapel was kindly availed to me for worship with my students. My outreach on these four campuses was in lunch meetings in the cafeteria. This was a good chance to meet students and invite them to our programs.

The search committee that called me to the Diocese of West Tennessee had anticipated that I could have drawn students from all the four colleges to come to joint ministries at Barth House. It did not take me long to realize that each of the four colleges had a different ethos that would not allow the type of ministry arrangement anticipated by the search committee. In addition, college competition deterred the pursuit of that kind of arrangement. I, therefore, chose not to push the arrangement and instead organized programs in each of the four colleges. Nevertheless, I still managed to persuade students from the other three colleges to participate in some joint activities such as Thanksgiving dinner and occasional Sunday evening Holy Eucharist services and dinner at Barth House. There were also times when we got together for community service, mission and conferences.

A typical multi-campus program for
me was scheduled as follows:

Monday	Office day and Campus visitation Bible study – CBU
Tuesday	Office day, preparation of Bible study and sermon.

Wednesday	Holy Eucharist and lunch – Barth House, U of M
	Holy Eucharist – Rhodes College - 6:00 P.M.
Thursday	Noon Prayer - Christian Brothers University
	Bible study – Barth House - 7:00 PM
Friday	Bible Study – LeMoyne-Owen – 12.00 Noon
Saturday	Day off and the usual church meetings
Sunday	Holy Eucharist service and dinner - Barth House
	Compline – Rhodes College - facilitated by students

It sure was a very loaded schedule, but it was also most fulfilling.

Canterbury House

One of the popular names used for college ministry is Canterbury Club, no doubt drawn from the Canterbury, the seat of the Archbishop of Canterbury, the head of the Anglican Church. The tradition goes as far back as Archbishop Cranmer who was himself a college chaplain before finally becoming Archbishop. Although Episcopal student organizations have readily described themselves as Canterbury Club, the name Canterbury House is technically used to describe a large Episcopal house designated for college ministry. Most of these houses were built during the times of Church affluence and vision, to cater to college ministry. Canterbury Houses are, therefore, within the proximity of the campus. They are Church owned and run. Canterbury Houses are havens for students' relaxation and reflection especially for groups of students that may feel threatened in one way or other. Normally these are multi-purpose buildings, which may contain offices, meeting rooms, kitchens, residential space for either staff or students, and of course a worshiping space. Students and staff living in Canterbury House pay minimal rent to enable the upkeep of the property. Some students perform certain duties like cleaning or peer ministry in lieu of rent or portion of their rent.

Normally, the college chaplain also assumes the role of the director of the Canterbury House and all the responsibilities pertaining to that office. It is from this house that the chaplain conducts worship services and Bible study among other programs that the chaplain may have.

Lay-led College Ministry Model

Yet another model of college ministry is lay led. There are some gifted church members who deeply care for college students. Some of these are faculty and staff in our colleges. Others are members of the local parish who feel called to work with college students. Others are lay people who have gone through seminary and, for whatever reason, have not been ordained, and yet feel called to work with college students. Some of these lay ministers are tent makers. They do college ministry alongside their other employment. Others are paid to do this ministry by the diocese.

In spite of their limitations, there are many lay college chaplains who do a commendable job working with students. Sometimes lay ministers coordinate with the local clergy to come and celebrate the Holy Eucharist on a regular basis. Either way, the lay-led college ministry is a viable model that may be suitable in certain situations. This model, of course, has limitations in that in a very liturgical church, the lay college chaplain cannot celebrate the sacraments. It is, therefore, not surprising to see many of those lay college chaplains enter seminary to train and be ordained as priests.

Peer Ministry Model

Related to the lay-led model of college ministry is the peer ministry. Peer ministry is led by a student or group of students who have been instructed in the hows of doing this ministry. There are students who readily relate well to the peer ministers. For one, the peer minister is one of them. There is a commonality and understanding that, properly handled has the potential to build rapport between the peer minister and other students. The peer ministers are contracted by the diocese, the parish, or by a college chaplain, to reach out to fellow students. Usually their compensation includes free room and board and a small stipend. Some peer ministries have worked well while others have not done so well. There is always the potential of liability if things are not well handled and the peer minister is not well supervised. There have been cases of alcohol and sex abuse in religious houses. But I must quickly point out that such abuses are not limited to peer ministries. Other college ministry models have suffered these experiences. Some of the more successful peer ministries are those contracted and supervised by an active college chaplain. Peer ministry therefore complements that of the full time college chaplain. With all its limitations, the peer ministry is a viable model that may be suitable for some dioceses striving to keep the doors of their Canterbury House open.

Tent-Making Model

The Tent-Making Model is neither often heard of nor very popular in the Episcopal Church, but I suggest that this model is also worth trying. Looking back on my ministry, I have come full cycle. I have discussed above how I began ministering to high school students as their *de facto* chaplain. My paid job was to teach but in addition, as all baptized Christians are called to do, I found a cause that I identified with - reaching out to students in their spiritual lives. This was the model that began at Barth House. I have described above how the teachers at what was then known as Memphis Normal School hatched a vision to minister to the spiritual needs of their students. This was a non-stipendiary ministry. They were tent makers who hatched a vision and supported it with their time and resources.

Since leaving my paid job as college chaplain in the Diocese of West Tennessee, I have been a tent-maker in college ministry. The Lord blessed us with a facility at 672 Alabama Avenue. We have continued to gather there for worship services on Sundays. We have been ministering to students attending school at the University of Memphis, Crichton College, LeMoyne-Owen College, Rust College,

Southwest Community College and others institutions of higher learning in the greater Memphis area. Again, I have to say that this is not a very popular model these days, but it has worked. If it is the last alternative, this model is worth trying as a stop-gap ministry at the U of M rather than continue to have the facility closed all together. I realize that there are accountability-related issues but we must not allow these kinds of hindrances to prevent us do what is right.

To summarize, college ministry models come in all kinds and sizes. No "one size fits all" model can be prescribed for all college campuses. What works in one college or situation may not necessarily work in another. Similarly, as the saying goes "If it isn't broken, do not fix it." There is no point in changing one model of college ministry for another just for the sake of it. On the other hand, it is counter-productive to insist on a model that is obviously a non-starter. Results from such an undertaking may be disastrous. Regular evaluations, preferably by the College Ministry Board will ensure whether or not the model in place is on track or not.

Chapter Four

College Ministry Board

"For as in one body we have many members, and all the members do not have the same function, so we, though many, are one body in Christ, and individually members one of another." (Rom. 12:4-5)

Support for Campus Minister

It is vitally important that the Diocesan leadership establish a college ministry board to serve with the college chaplain or chaplains. College ministry can be a lonely job, lonely in that unlike the parish where the rector has a vestry and a chain of committees to work with, college ministry is often a one-person show. To be sure, this is not how it should be, but more often than not, this is the case. In my particular case, whereas there was a search committee established to look for a college chaplain for the Diocese of West Tennessee, there was no College Ministry Board established to work with the chaplain. Fortunately, I was coming from the Diocese of Massachusetts where I had been a member of an active college works committee that regularly met at 40 Prescott Street, Brookline, to deliberate on college ministry affairs for universities in the Boston area. The committee included chaplains from Boston University, Northeastern University, Harvard University, MIT, Tufts University, Leslie College, among others. This board gave much needed moral support for active chaplains.

College Ministry Board

One of my requests to the search committee that called me to the Diocese of West Tennessee was that they work with me in finding my way in Memphis. The committee agreed to do so and they were, on the whole, most helpful. But I also knew that for that kind of help to be ongoing, the committee needs to be constituted and have the support of Diocesan authorities. I, therefore, identified one of my first tasks in my new job as one of establishing an active College Ministry Board with a clear job description. Board membership had to be wide enough as to include, faculty and staff from respective colleges, student representatives, diocesan representatives, and as much as possible, clergy representatives. Diverse college ministry composition ensures that the chaplain or chaplains have enough support or liaisons to facilitate their work.

Job Description

I was fortunate to be coming from a diocese where we had a clear job description for the college works committee. I did not have to reinvent the wheel so to speak. I readily used my experience and resources to come up with a job description for members of the College Ministry Board in the Diocese of West Tennessee. This job description included:

1. To serve as an advisory body to the college chaplain(s) in the Diocese
2. To review the mission statement of college ministry in the diocese from time to time
3. To provide support for college chaplain(s) in the ongoing work of campus ministries.
4. To work with the college chaplain in articulating a clear vision and models for college ministry in the diocese.
5. To promote college ministry throughout the diocese by educating communicants on the importance of this ministry.
6. To support and strengthen college ministries at the University of Memphis, Rhodes College, Christian Brothers University and LeMoyne-Owen College.
7. To explore ways and means of expanding college ministry to other institutions of higher education in the diocese.
8. To identify, nurture, develop and take an informing role in the selection of capable chaplains for campus ministry; encourage candidates for holy orders to consider vocation in campus ministry.
9. To advocate for campus ministry in ensuring that there is sufficient diocesan financial support for college chaplain(s), programs

> for the Barth House Center and other new campus ministries.
> 10. To develop and apply criteria for evaluating campus ministries on a regular basis and to ensure accountability for the college chaplain in the performance of his/her work.

I approached Bishop Coleman with this job description. With the help of some of the members of the search committee I had already met and come to trust, I picked names of representative people to constitute my first College Ministry Board. I gave these names to Bishop Coleman for his official invitation for them to constitute the board. The Bishop gladly did this and I had my first College Ministry Board.

The job description of the College Ministry Board may vary in some degree or other from one college setting to another. But a close examination of these responsibilities will show that, all things being equal, the establishment of an active College Ministry Board simplifies the work of the college chaplain. It makes him/her accountable and, at the same time, defuses some of the pressure that may come to bear on the chaplain in his/her performance of college ministry. Unfortunately, some College Ministry Boards are weak. Others are not fully recognized by the diocesan leadership and, therefore, lack the necessary voice to perform their responsibilities. The opposite may be equally true. An overly strong board may get in the way of the chaplain's performance of his/her work. A balance needs to be maintained. Either way, it is very important that the diocesan bishop recognize and endorse the role of the College Ministry Board.

Recognition of the College Ministry Board

My particular experience is that for the College Ministry Board to successfully discharge its role as outlined in the job description a few things need to happen.

a) The board must be mandated and, as much as possible, be elected by the Diocesan Convention. This high level diocesan recognition assures legitimacy and much needed support from the diocesan authorities.

b) The board needs the support of the Diocesan Bishop to whom it will regularly report. On the other hand the diocesan bishop needs to support and provide autonomy to the College Ministry Board in performing its work.

c) The board needs to have its own chairperson who is committed to college ministry. It is the responsibility of the chair of the College Ministry Board to convene regular meetings in consultation with the chaplain, who in most cases serves as the secretary to the board.

d) The board must include as many constituencies of the diocese as possible. This inclusive representation will ensure wide support, both financial and moral, for the ongoing work of college ministry.

The Rev. Dr. Samson N. Gitau

Fund Raising

One primary role for the College Ministry Board is to raise financial support for college ministry. The finances generated from these efforts will support the chaplain(s) and ministry programs. It is not uncommon to have this role dumped on the laps of the college minister in addition to his/her day to day busy schedule. This trend may end up in burn out for the college chaplain or cause a feeling of disinterest and lack of support from the rest of the Diocesan population. The trend will also inevitably affect the day to day programming of the chaplain.

To avoid these problems, the College Ministry Board must step up to the plate and do its job of providing support for the college minister and his/her ministry. An active College Ministry Board advocates for college ministry, the chaplain and the young adults of the Church. It's the board's primary responsibility to put college ministry at the forefront of church authorities and their financial budgets and decisions. It's their job to ensure that the college chaplain is given sufficient resources to do what he/she is called to do. Without sufficient programming support, the chaplain is limited in what he/she can do.

One way of supporting the college minister is for members of the College Ministry Board to regularly participate in college ministry programs especially worship. This allows board members to see first-hand what is going on in college ministry. It also allows the students to meet and interact with their benefactors. But perhaps the most important role of the College Ministry Board is in its involvement in the ongoing financial support of college ministry.

Pitfalls

The most ideal method of funding college ministry is through a line item in the Diocesan budget. This method has the advantage of freeing the college chaplain or chaplains to concentrate on their programs with the students. The Diocesan budget itself is derived from a combination of a variety of sources, including parish asking, investments and bequeaths. In Dioceses where college ministry is a priority, it is not hard to find this funding. The Bishop and the diocesan councils already know that college ministry is a priority. They will, therefore, do all they can to ensure that funding is available. However, in those dioceses where college ministry is either an afterthought, incidental or half-hearted ministry, getting the necessary funding may be an uphill climb.

As already pointed out, one of the roles of the College Ministry Board is to ensure that college ministry is adequately funded. A strong and representative board will ensure that this role is fulfilled as board members will assert their influence in the relevant diocesan committees, such as the board of finance and Bishop and Council, among others. In fact, where college ministry is a priority of the diocese, such cajoling may not even be necessary, since almost everybody is well aware of the importance of this ministry.

There are at least two disadvantages for being wholly funded from the diocesan budget. First, in the event the diocesan asking falls short, more often than not, college ministry will be first in line to be cut as already pointed out. College ministry must be set in a way that ensures that it is not at the mercy of a few decision makers but rather the project of the majority of the diocesan populace. The second disadvantage is that the college minister and his/her ministry may tend to be overly muzzled by the diocesan office. Unfortunately, and as much as one would hate to admit, this is often the case.

The most ideal and helpful situation is for college ministry to be funded from a combination of the diocesan budget, parish and some endowment. This kind of arrangement ensures continuity and support from a variety of sources. It also ensures ownership of the supporters.

Parish Support

As already pointed out above, financial support for parish-based model of college ministry comes directly from the parish budget. This in return is derived from membership pledges, bequeaths and, in some cases, endowments. Some of these endowments may be restricted to college ministry. The parish-funded college ministry has the advantage of ownership by the parish populace. Usually, the college is in the parish neighborhood, with some of the faculty and staff from this institution attending church in this parish. It is also often the case that the parish has prior history with the institution. The parish, therefore, enjoys the natural connection with the college and readily assumes ongoing responsibility to fund this college ministry. Sometimes, the college chaplain is a member of the parish staff with the designated responsibility to college ministry. Thus, members of the parish may take pride identifying with this ministry. This pride may translate into financial support for college ministry.

Alumni Bank

Some of the most successful campus ministries in terms of funding are those whose alumni are engaged in their financial support. After all, almost every college relies on its alumni for ongoing fund raising. The success of this method requires the college chaplain and his/her staff to keep an alumni bank. This bank will be comprised of students who have actively participated and benefited from college ministry. These alumni know first hand what college ministry means to them. Keeping and maintaining an alumni bank is an ongoing work. The bank must be regularly updated.

The alumni bank may also include parents of college ministry alumni. Some parents are most grateful that their children found a home away from home. Some of these parents well know that college ministry was in part responsible in retaining their children in college when the going was tough. Some of these parents become regular donors to college ministry when their children are going through school. Their names should be kept and regularly invited to give donations to support college ministry.

The most effective way of reaching out to the alumni and parents is through a regular newsletter. This is comparable to the parish newsletter. The newsletter highlights events in college ministry, outlines the plans ahead and the challenges facing this ministry.

An enclosed envelop will usually make it easier for an alumnus to make his/her donation to college ministry. It is important for the college chaplain to send a thank you note to each donor for any donation received, big or small.

Dinners

Other methods of fund raising for campus ministry are similar to those used in parishes. They include dinners, with so much charged per plate. A lot of work goes into the actual planning for this kind of event. The more people involved in this process the better. It is a way of promoting the ministry. It also gives a sense of ownership. Involvement of college students in these activities is most desirable. It gives the students a sense of ownership also. The more the students are involved in the hands-on activities, the more likely they are to participate in the actual programming, and the more likely they are to tell other students about college ministry.

It helps a lot to have some members of the campus community pledge to this ministry. These members may include faculty and staff, College Ministry Board members, and the college ministry staff, including the college minister him/herself. Unless the college minister is a member of another local Church, college ministry ought to be the college minister's church. Like any other member of a church, the college minister has a responsibility to give regularly to this ministry. More so, if not for anything else, the college minister should pledge to this ministry as a way of demonstrating leadership. A leader who only tells others 'do as I say, but not what I do' will not succeed. A leader is one who knows the way, shows the way and goes the way him/herself.

Other Responsibilities for College Ministry Board

An active College Ministry Board meets regularly. This may be bimonthly or quarterly. In some cases, as in the parish-based model, the College Ministry Board should meet monthly just like a parish vestry. The college chaplain is usually the secretary to the College Ministry Board. He/she records the minutes and ensures that board members receive copies of these minutes in a timely fashion.

The board advocates for the college chaplain to all interested parties. Members of the board receive first hand information of the running of the college ministry. They are aware of the programs in place and the numbers of students participating in these programs. The board not only helps the chaplain raise the necessary funds for college ministry, but also keeps track of how these funds are expended. In some cases, this role may not be necessary, since the diocese may already have put in place a better method of ensuring accountability for college ministry funds. Either way, the College Ministry Board consists of the supporting battalion to ensure success in college ministry.

Chapter Five

College Ministry Programming

And his gifts were that some should be apostles, some prophets, some evangelists, some pastors and teachers, to equip the saints for the work of ministry, for building up the body of Christ." (Eph. 4:11-12)

Facility

Barth House at the corner of Patterson and Watauga Avenue

Barth House Welcomes you

The Barth House property located at 409 Patterson Street has one of the best chapels at the University of Memphis. It's ideal for worship and small weddings. However, the facility lacks room for student recreation such as ping pong and pool table, amenities available to most other religious houses at the University of Memphis.

The expansion of the Barth House facility to cater to these amenities was my dream. I had talked to Bishop Johnson about this dream and even submitted blueprints for this purpose. The expectation was that if Barth House could be extended frontward toward Patterson Street, it would give us a large room for student recreation. An additional floor would provide the facility with student residential rooms comparable to the Methodist and Roman Catholic student centers at the University of Memphis. This addition would greatly enhance the Episcopal college ministry. My vision was to write grants to raise money for this purpose. The diocese could also include Barth House in its proposed capital campaign. Great things start with a dream. Although some of our dreams may end up in disappointment, we must never stop dreaming.

Mission

Like any other organization, college ministry must have a mission. The mission defines the reason to be for a particular ministry. It is an ongoing goal setter that seeks to address the needs of an organization. The mission helps maintain focus in the ministry. The mission of Barth House for the last nearly ten years has been:

To serve, support and equip students, staff and faculty to live and practice their faith in diverse campus communities and to worship and proclaim the Word of God by word and example.

All our college ministry programs are geared towards one purpose and one purpose only, that is, the implementation of our mission. At the end of the day, our goal is to be able to look back and say that we have equipped our students, staff and faculty to live their Christian lives and to practice their faith in a diverse campus. This was the primary reason for our being in college ministry. It was clearly outlined on the front page of the Barth House website. Our flyers and bulletins also carried this mission statement.

For most freshmen, college ministry is their first major experience away from home, parents, and friends. Some were well rooted and supported in their local youth groups. Some were most probably church goers who went to church mainly from a sense of obligation to please their parents. Coming to college exposes young adults to an entirely newfound freedom. Most are ready to make the best of this newfound freedom. One of the first things to fall away from their lives is church attendance. More often than not, if the church loses these young adults, we have lost them for a long time if not for ever. Those who come back do so when they have gone through college and are ready for marriage or ready to raise families. Then the church may become an option. But for those that we are able to get in college, their spiritual life is mainly uninterrupted. Instead, it gets stronger and healthier. Oftentimes, it is from this group that some realize the call to the ordained ministry.

Our role in college ministry is to take off from where the youth directors have stopped. That is why it is important for college ministers to work closely with youth directors. The latter can be most helpful in introducing college freshmen to college chaplains. In return, college chaplains follow-up with these freshmen. The college chaplain's primary responsibility is to nurture students and to equip them for responsible and fruitful Christian life. The role of the college chaplain is to lead the young adults in owning their faith. When this goal is fully realized, then the young adults can say "I no longer do this for my parents; I do it for myself and for the love of God."

Campus ministry programming is, of course, the meat of college ministry. No matter how beautiful and spacious the college ministry amenities, without good and attractive programming these amenities are useless.

What exactly do we do in college ministry? Just as there is a wide variety of colleges and ethos, college ministry programming must also be tailored to suit a particular college and its ethos. Each college ministry may have one or two signature programs. Some colleges will do very well with worship services, others in community services and yet others in Bible studies. It is also important to note that what worked yesterday may not work today. Program variation is desirable just as a good teacher seeks to vary his/her method of teaching. At Barth House, we sought to offer a wide variety of programs in an attempt to reach out to both commuter as well as residential students. Some of the programs that we did over the years included:

Worship

The Episcopal Church is best known for its rich liturgy. It is important, therefore, that campus ministry engages in some worship service of one type or another. At Barth House, we had two primary Holy Eucharist worship services on Sundays and Wednesdays at 6:00 P.M. and 11:30 A.M. respectively. Each of the two services was followed by a home-cooked meal and fellowship. Fellowship was especially very enriching on Sundays when most students were more relaxed and not running from class to class as was the case on Wednesdays. The relaxed mood was ideal for conversation with students on contemporary issues facing the Church or the nation or college.

The Rev. Dr. Samson N. Gitau

It is important for students to be actively involved both in the preparation and actual conduct of worship. A student-led college ministry choir particularly made this participation more meaningful. Students also took turns in reading the Sunday lessons. A few of them served as LEMs. Others served as acolytes, and in a few cases, I recruited and worked with some students to deliver homilies. This was particularly suitable on Talent Sunday, when I invited students to share their talents. This hands-on liturgical participation by students is very appealing to other students who see their colleagues vested and actively participating in worship leadership. College ministry worship is a students' worship service and, therefore, students should be involved in its preparation and conduct. Educators will concur that there is no better way of teaching than the hands-on method. The same principle and practice availed in our worship services at Rhodes College and CBU.

Students are more open to experimentation and new ideas. As part of this process we sometimes experimented with a variety of Eucharistic forms ranging from A to D in the Book of Common Prayer. We also experimented with Rite I and II, in addition to other liturgies from other Anglican Provinces such as Kenya and New Zealand. Most students appreciated exposure to these other worship forms.

The sermon is a primary component of the campus worship experience. Most of my sermons are purposely didactic and thematic. My stated goal was to lead the students to own their faith. As already pointed out, there are many students who until now went to Church because their parents said they do so. They basically professed the faith of their parents. But now in college, it is important that the students own their faith. It is important that they come to church not to please their parents, but because it gives them the necessary connection with God.

Bible study

Bible study was one of our signature programs in college ministry. We now have a generation that has not read or studied the Bible. If they missed going to Sunday school, most young adults failed to have this necessary exposure to the Bible. It took me a while to fully comprehend the magnitude of this problem at the U of M. I would go to class and make a statement such as: "As you know in the story of Abraham, when he was asked by God to go and sacrifice his son Isaac...." Students would stare at me with blank faces. It was not until one student openly said to me "Dr. Gitau, we do not know these stories." This was an eye opener for me. I have since learned not to take anything for granted. College ministry is a fertile ground for evangelism. It is the new frontier for mission. The Church must wake up to this realization and heed the words of Jesus that "the harvest is plenty, but the laborers are few." The Church has an obligation to recruit, deploy and support laborers in this ready vineyard of our campuses. Like the old missionary societies such as the CMS and others, the Church must send missionaries to this mission field because it the right thing to do.

In the course of my ten years of college ministry, I have taken Bible study very seriously. Bible study is the way to equip the people of God for ministry. It is the way to nurture souls. It is the sure way to discernment. Yes, discernment on who one is, who one desires to be and what God is calling one to do. Bible study is the path to discovery, not only of oneself but also of the wonderful plan that God has for each one us, especially for our youth. In an age of plurality and numerous heresies floating all around, Bible study is the sure way of discerning the truth. This is more so with young adults who are more prone and open to new ideas. Delving deep in the word of God leads one to better and more informed decisions in life.

Throughout these years I have taught Bible study courses on Mark, Luke, John, Romans, Thessalonians, Galatians, Revelation, Pastoral Letters, and Book of Psalms, to name some. I have taught Bible study courses at University of Memphis, Christian Brothers University and LeMoyne-Owen College. The class meets weekly for one hour. My method of doing Bible study is by engaging students in dialogue. The Bible study is not another homily, but a time of exploration, questing, discussion and affirmation.

Baptism and Confirmation Classes

As the new frontier for evangelism, college ministry provides opportunities for reaching out to entirely new Christian converts. Surprisingly, some students neither got the opportunity to attend Sunday school, nor even got baptized or confirmed. This could be in part because their parents did not themselves go to church or did not find it important to take their children to participate in Christian services and teachings. In talking with some college students, it is not uncommon to find out that some of them are not baptized. Others are not confirmed. But of those who may have been baptized as infants, many never got the opportunity to go through the church teaching as to why we do the things that we do. In other situations, a student may have been baptized in another denomination and in coming to the Episcopal Church finds it attractive and wishes to be confirmed in the faith of this Church.

Each year we conducted baptism or confirmation classes for students seeking these services. The classes give us the opportunity to go through Catechism, also known as the Outline of the Faith. It gives us the opportunity to take the students through the Baptismal Covenant, the Apostles and Nicene Creeds, the Sacraments of the Church, Holy Scriptures, Worship, to name a few of these topics. More often than not, these classes are eye-openers to the students. Even for those who may have been confirmed at an early age, these classes provoke new insights in the teaching of the Church.

The Rev. Dr. Samson N. Gitau

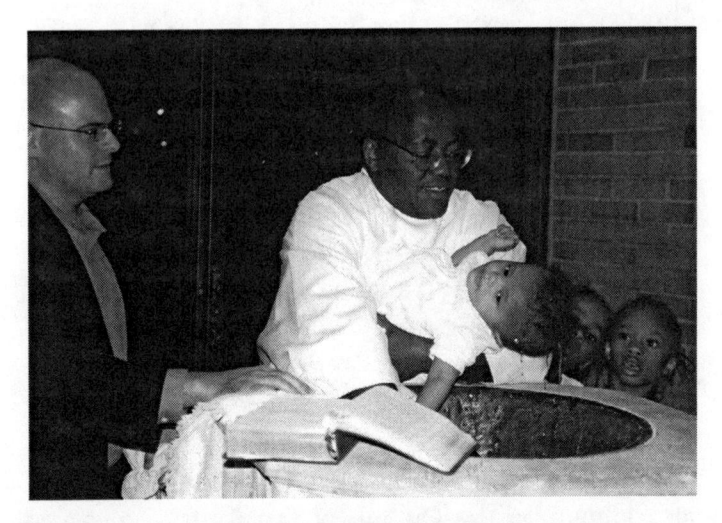

Baptism at Barth House

Bishop James Coleman confirms three candidates at Barth House

Pitfalls

Marriage

College ministry is also a forum of fellowship and socialization. Whereas the campus has no paucity of parties and other forums where students get together, some of these parties are wild and unhealthy to students wishing to preserve their integrity. Religious houses provide safe havens for students to meet and socialize. It is not uncommon for romantic relationships to develop from such encounters. There are many couples who testify how they met in college ministry and ended up getting married.

It is always a delight to see young adults who meet in college ministry and have their love grow and develop into a real commitment. In cases like this, it is not uncommon for such students to come to the college chaplain for premarital counseling and solemnization of their marriage. At Barth House, I conducted one or two student marriages each year. It is a great joy to work with the parents of such students to facilitate the wedding of their children.

Abby and Josh tie the knot at Barth House

The Rev. Dr. Samson N. Gitau

Counseling

Unfortunately, in other cases some of these relationships fail to develop to full maturity. Broken relationships are quite common in college life. Student counseling in this area is a primary component of student counseling in general. In some of these cases, one of the parties or even both parties are hurt by a broken relationship and in some cases, a broken engagement. My role as college chaplain is to be there for hurting students. It is to encourage them to look for the silver lining beyond the broken relationship. In some cases, the aggrieved party is hurt enough to contemplate suicide. It is not uncommon to have one or two college student suicides each year. When this happens, it is most devastating to the campus community. Our motto in Religious Life Staff is that 'life has meaning.' In my ministry of encouragement, I invite the hurting student to know that life has meaning beyond a broken relationship. I invite the students to know that God has a wonderful plan for their lives. I encourage them to know that God often takes away a makeshift, only to give us a mansion. I do not say this to belittle the student's hurt, but to have them know that God and God's plans for us are bigger than what has happened. I seek to have the student learn from the life lesson of the past, but at the same time focus in the future.

Another area of student counseling has to do with their academic performance. Most students, of course, worry about their grades. Some worry because they know that their scholarships are contingent upon their attainment of certain GPAs. Others worry because they have a contract with their parents. And yet others worry

Pitfalls

because they have set certain goals and expectations for themselves. So when some of these students fall short of their goals and expectations, they are devastated. They need to talk to someone.

As adjunct professor at the University of Memphis, my experience comes in handy in dealing with these kinds of students. I know firsthand that most professors are readily willing to work with students to pass their classes or to improve on their grades. Some professors give make-up quizzes and essays. The crucial thing is for students to ensure that they show genuine interest and commitment to their classes. It is important that students make themselves known to their teachers and let them know where they need help. When this happens, most professors will work with students to reach their desired goals.

Unfortunately, students are notorious for procrastination. Others think that good grades are deserved handouts. My experience at the University of Memphis is that students are notorious for absenteeism to an extent I have yet to see elsewhere. It is not uncommon to see a student absent him/herself for five or even six classes in a course and yet expect to get a good grade or pass in that class. Good grades are to be earned. Every professor wants to have hard working students in his/her class. So in counseling students in their academic performance, I seek to show the student their responsibility and what they need to do to get to where they want to go. Other students are on the verge of giving up. I encourage such students not to give up, but instead to take a lesser load the following semester and also to take summer courses to catch up where they may have fallen behind or in order to accelerate their program. The university has all kinds of student help. There are counselors available to help the students. But some students will hesitate to make use of this help. A talk with a college chaplain affirming the student's potential may be all that it takes to reorient the student back on track.

One of the roles of the college chaplain is to be available for student crises. Student crises may be a result of attempted suicides, accidents, theft, over-drinking, fights or students involved in crimes. Whereas some of these are clear-cut police cases, others are counseling opportunities that require the intervention of the college chaplain.

In some cases, I have played the role of student advocate. In one case a student was summoned for disciplinary hearing and needed someone to stand by her. This student had under-performed in her teaching practicum. The supervisor concluded that the student teacher was unable to maintain discipline in class. The authorities had concluded that the student was unfit to be a teacher. I accompanied the student to the hearing and tried my best to advocate for her. She was determined to be an elementary school teacher. Even though the hearing did not go very well for this student, I was there for her and used my knowledge of the hearing to help her later. She adjusted her major and acquired enough credits to graduate. This story had a happy ending. This student never gave up her dream. She went on to look for a job as a teacher. She applied for a masters' program. I recall with much joy the day this student called me in my office to let me know that she had not only passed her master's program but had also been certified to teach. My small role in this process was well worth it.

In another case, a student was caught with a gun in the dorm. This was obviously a police case. The student was indicted for illegal possession of a gun and, no doubt, other issues. The student was known to me. I knew that he came from a Christian background and was just being rebellious. The crime was bad. But I also believed that this student, like any other repentant person, could reform. He could go back to school and graduate. At this student's and parents' request, I wrote a letter of support to the presiding judge. The student was released on the promise of good conduct. Unfortunately, this story did not have an immediate happy ending. My role was to be there for the student and, in this case, his parents. I hope that one day this student will look back to this case with gratitude in his life.

Ecumenism

College ministry provides an opportunity for ecumenism. Up to when they enter college as freshmen, most students have only known their own church. Some of their parents have jealously shielded them from any and all other denominations. Some of these young adults have been home-schooled to ensure proper quarantine from denominational and other spiritual and social "viruses." While the intentions may be good, sometimes this leads to unsupportable ignorance of the faith of other people. Many times I have introduced myself to students with words: "I am the Episcopal Chaplain in this school." To which a student often says something like: "Are you Christians?" or "What is that?"

Unfortunately, this ignorance is not limited to college students. It pervades to faculty and staff also. I recall one of my visits to LeMoyne-Owen where I met Dr. Okamolafi, a professor of political science and a native of Nigeria. I introduced myself as the new Episcopal chaplain to which he asked me what denomination that was. When I told him about the historical connection between the Episcopal Church and the Anglican Church and that I was myself an Anglican priest from Kenya, his eyes beamed and he said, "I am also an Anglican from Nigeria." I suddenly realized the hindrance our sign name at Barth House was likely to cause. I went back to my office and had the sign changed to read "Episcopal/Anglican Church. From then on international students started frequenting our programs. Those who were Anglicans readily identified with us and the programs we offered.

At the University of Memphis, we have a recognized department of Religious Life Staff. Members of this organization are the full-time college chaplains and directors of religious houses. The RLS at the U of M is a good model for other college ministries. Participating denominations and religions included: Episcopalians, Church of Christ, Presbyterians, Methodists, Baptists, Roman Catholics, Jewish and, sometimes, even Muslims. A few other denominations participated in some of our programs even though they had neither full-time staff nor their own religious houses. Recognition of a religious life department in a public college is not to be taken for

Pitfalls

granted. But I believe that the university leadership knows and acknowledges the indispensable service rendered by religious life staff to the college community. It is an established fact that the retention rate for students who are engaged in college activities is much higher than for those who are not. College ministry is one practical way to engage students. Students find much needed support from college ministry in the pursuit of their academic goals.

Some of our joint programs in religious life included monthly meetings where we talked about what is going on in campus and how to participate. We shared what was going on in our individual religious life houses and what programs were working or not working. In these talks, we were able to identify some of the religious house-hopping students. These are students who are in the habit of hopping from one religious house to another with no commitment to any of them. Sometimes this trend could be all right and actually encouraged, but there are other times when some of these students are troublemakers, who tend to make others uncomfortable with how they conduct themselves. In other cases, these religious house-hoppers are non-students, carrying backpacks and a few books, to pass as students for a free meal or place to hang out. Sharing with one another enables college chaplains to identify and deal with these impostors.

In terms of actual programming, some of our most successful programs in religious life included the freshman move-in. Each religious house formed a team to help the freshmen and their parents move stuff into the dorms. This, of course, takes place in the summer when it is very hot. Parents and the freshmen appreciate this help very much. For the religious life teams, this is also an opportunity to make ourselves known to both the freshmen and their parents without necessarily appearing to proselytize. It is a case of preaching the gospel without words. The conspicuous name tags won by participants convey the message.

Progressive Dinners

Joint progressive dinners, starting with salad in one religious house, continuing with main course in another house, and finishing with dessert in yet another, attracted many students. This program also gave each college chaplain the chance to introduce themselves and their programs to the students. The progressive dinners were often spiced up with prizes from each religious house with a grand prize at the last house. Sometimes we gave out mugs engraved with the names and addresses of each religious house.

The Biblical foods sampling program is also a draw to students. This was staged on the main campus and included almost every food mentioned in the Bible. Students were keen to sample these free foods. The forum also gave each director of a religious house the chance to give out their flyers to interested students with an invitation to come try their programs. Camel rides sponsored by the Jewish Student Union made the program even more attractive with each student seeking to have his/her picture taken riding on the camel.

September 11

One of the most successful joint religious life programs was a prayer meeting following the September 11 attack. Like almost everybody else in the country, the students were apprehensive and fearful of what had happened. They were obviously anxious about what would happen next. Gathering together Jewish, Muslims, Christians from all our religious houses, with each one of us either leading a prayer or reading a portion of scripture, sent a very powerful message. The Religious Life Staff is here to help. It also sent a message that we are in this together. The event was attended by more than 500 students. This is the kind of thing that no one religious life house can accomplish on its own. Jointly, we presented a voice and message that the whole university community appreciated. The event was meant to encourage the students. There was no doubt that we managed to reach that goal.

However, one incident stood out and still stands out for me from this occasion. Participating from the Jewish Student Union were Elaina and Nabil from the Muslim Students' Union. Nabil had come with his two young boys about seven and nine years old. They were sitting next to me. Each one of us directors of religious life had the opportunity to introduce ourselves and our religious houses. When Elaina introduced herself and said that she was Jewish, Nabil's nine-year-old turned to his father and audibly said, "Dad, she said that she is Jewish." It was obvious that the two young boys were uncomfortable with what they had heard. The father was embarrassed from the rather unexpected reaction and discomfort of his young boys. He turned to the boys and said "Yes, her name is Elaina - she is Jewish but she is a good person." If nothing else happened that day, the sideshow for me was even more meaningful than the primary program we were there to do.

New Student Orientations

One of the many ways we sought to reach out to the new students is in the new student orientation, organized by the University. Different organizations and departments host information tables where flyers and other handouts are given to the freshmen and their parents. The University kindly involves us in these orientations. The religious life staff takes turns with at least two persons representing the others in handing out religious life materials. Most important in these handouts is a religious life survey card with the names of all the denominations represented at the University. We ask the freshmen to fill out this card. Blow pops often do the trick to entice students to fill out the religious life survey card. The cards are then sorted out and each religious life staff gets those that belong to his/her denomination. It is up to each chaplain to follow-up with these freshmen inviting them to scheduled programs. Oftentimes, some students fill out "non-denominational." In such a case, any religious life staff is welcome to use the information to invite the non-denominational students to their programs.

The new student orientation program provides the religious life staff a forum for working together. The staff is not into sheep stealing, but working together. We encourage students who belong to a given denomination to participate in the activities of their religious houses. At the same time, we maintain an open door for any and all students, who wish to participate in activities of a particular religious house.

Sometimes, religious life staffs team together in a shared program. At the University of Memphis, The Rivers Edge (United Methodists) and the Presbyterian Place teamed together for many years in a joint Bible study. One year, I teamed together with the Roman Catholic Chaplain in a Bible study on the Gospel of Mark. Another year the Presbyterian chaplain and I teamed together for Wednesday Holy Eucharist services. Several times, I invited Mr. Ken Pfhol, the Presbyterian chaplain, to give a homily at Barth House.

Mission Trip

The most successful ministry that we shared with the Presbyterian Place was a joint mission trip to Kenya in May, 2006. We took a group of ten students on a mission trip to Kenya, where we worked in an irrigation project, digging trenches, laying PVC pipes to assist small farmers to grow passion fruit. We also took medical supplies for a health center in my home village in Central Kenya. Working and worshiping together created strong bonds that have continued long after the mission trip. We have since made another trip with my Presbyterian colleague to build a high school in Kenya.

Other ecumenical projects are local. For several years, we teamed together as the religious life staff to provide shelter and food for homeless persons who had recently lost their jobs. The primary objective in this program was to enable these persons get another job. But for us and our students, the program provided an opportunity with which most students were unfamiliar. I recall inviting one of our Barth House students to work with us in one of the homeless projects. She consulted her mother before consenting. The mother was a bit reluctant to let her daughter take part in this project. The mother's question to her daughter was "Jenny, what do you know about homelessness?" Precisely the point! The program provided Jenny and other students in her situation, much needed exposure to the needs of the city of Memphis where homelessness is a big problem.

Working together gives college chaplains and their students mutual respect and understanding of their religious backgrounds. It is an opportunity to explore what we have in common. One would hope that this kind of respect cultivated in college ministry would be replicated to foster ecumenical ties in other institutions of higher learning and seminaries.

Working together as religious life staff presented us with a powerful forum to air our concerns to the university. The Dean of Students was particularly interested in the affairs of Religious Life Staff. He regularly attended our monthly RLS meetings. He also invited the chair of religious life to his monthly staff meetings. The dean included the Religious Life Staff in his mailing list to inform them about the day-to-day working of the University. I was honored to serve for two terms as president of the Religious Life Staff at the U of M.

Barth House/Presbyterian Place missioners at BTL, Kenya

Trust in Ecumenical Settings

Establishing trust is crucial in doing college ministry especially for chaplains working in denominationally affiliated colleges other than their own. This was my experience when I was newly come to serve at CBU and Rhodes College. I recall how the directors of college ministry that I encountered both at CBU and Rhodes College at first looked at me with suspicion when I introduced myself to them as the new Episcopal chaplain in their colleges. It took a bit of time to establish trust but when it happened in both colleges, it became much easier to do my programs in the two colleges. At CBU I was soon honored with the invitation to give the commencement invocation. Later we even shared what is known as Intergenerational Bible study on Monday evenings with Brother Rob. I joined in some of the Roman Catholic worship programs. They even forgot that I was an Episcopalian and freely included me in their Holy Communion. In return, I invited both Sister Delores and Brother Rob for programs at Barth House. At Rhodes College, we soon teamed together for joint Ash Wednesday and Thanksgiving services. When trust is established, we all come to realize that we are there to complement each other in our ministries.

CBU Bible Study group

Diversity

The Episcopal Church is one of the most segregated Churches in the US. I have heard it defined as: "upper middle class white Church." To be sure, the Episcopal Church is very much into outreach. Episcopalians are very much into such community programs as helping

Pitfalls

Katrina victims, homeless shelters and soup kitchens. But the unspoken policy is: "stay where you are and we will bring you help there." As long as the needy keep to themselves, it will be all right. Any attempts to integrate with the marginalized, the poor, or persons that are different from themselves is much opposed. This is an uncomfortable fact to many good and caring Episcopalians. It is also a fact that has not escaped minorities. I remember introducing myself to some students at LeMoyne-Owen where I said that I was the Episcopal chaplain. Ricky, one of my Bible study students, asked me, "Fr. Samson, you said you are an Episcopalian; isn't that a white Church? How do they treat you there?" I had to once again explain the historical connection between the Episcopal Church and the Anglican Church of my background. It was news to Ricky and his friends for me to tell them that the membership and leadership of the Anglican Church in Africa is predominantly African. Right from its birthday on the Day of Pentecost, the church was meant to be diverse. Segregation for any Church is an anomaly. The reality with the Episcopal Church, however, is that attempts to bring about the much needed integration by some bold rectors have not only been strongly rebuffed by some churches, but sometimes members of these churches have resigned and gone to other churches. All this is in great contrast to the ever conspicuous red and blue Episcopal sign with the words, "the Episcopal Church welcomes you."

One of my goals in college ministry was to build an inclusive and diverse college community. At Barth House, we had students from India, China, Australia, Germany, England, and African countries such as Kenya,

The Rev. Dr. Samson N. Gitau

Ghana, Nigeria, Sudan, Sierra Leon and South Africa. We also had students from Latin America and of course, American students from a wide variety of states. Diversity was celebrated rather than looked down upon. Each student in college ministry brought something new to the community. I found myself quoting phrases from Susan, my Chinese student, as much as I was moved by Sara, my Asian Indian student, as she came forward to receive communion. I am persuaded that this is how it will look in heaven when God draws men and women from every corner of the earth and from every tribe and nation. God has no place for segregation.

Like any other college ministry, Barth House had its share of gay students. My policy in doing college ministry was simple – all were welcome but Barth House was not to be used as a forum for propagating sexual preferences. Jesus clearly set out the principle for us, "You will know the truth and the truth will set you free" (John 8:32). My policy was therefore not to be reactionary, but to preach the truth of the gospel and believe that its truth will set us free. Some gay students understood and supported this policy. They felt welcome and readily participated in the Barth House activities. A few did not. I recall one gay young man whom I had supported in a variety of ways and who often joined me in Morning Prayer. He offered to help me do a flyer to publicize our programs. I left him working on the project as I went to do a program at CBU. When I came back the young man had already finished the flyer and put up copies on the doors. The main emphasis of the flyer was that gay students were most welcome at Barth House. Whereas this was essentially true, I was opposed to singling out one particular sexual orientation and promoting it. I asked the young man to pull down the flyers and revise them. He was not happy with my decision. He left Barth House claiming that Barth House was unwelcoming to gay students. Any and all forms of discrimination are sinful, but the gospel of Jesus Christ demands the renewal of our lives.

Student Missions

A major gift with most young adults is the spirit of volunteerism. Young people want to help. With this gift is also the willingness to explore the world beyond their realm of living. Young people are adventurous. Mission work is therefore a natural program for college ministry. It is a "hands-on" learning experience that the students will never forget.

When we talk about mission today, most people will rush to the conclusion that it is the "haves" taking the goodies to the "have-nots." Such a concept of mission is most erroneous. It is based on the old colonial-missionary mentality of the civilized going to convert the heathens. Today, the Global South has become the center of Christendom. The Church in the Global South is growing more rapidly than the western world. Christians in the Global South take their faith very seriously. What they need is not conversion to Christianity. They already have that and even where that has not become a reality, the indigenous people are aware of it and are in a better position to evangelize their own. Instead, the people in the Global South are looking for partners in mission to partner with them in the projects they already have:

building churches, schools, health centers and foster homes, to name a few.

Mission is a mutual partnership. Each party has something to give as well as to receive. In planning mission trips for students, I make sure to emphasize this all-important reality. This concept of mutual partnership was hatched between churches in the 80s. It was called partner in mission (PIM). In undertaking our mission trips especially in the 21st century, we must bear this in mind. Oftentimes, the people who go out on mission end up getting more than they give. This is true for both local and international missions. So I ask my students to open their eyes and tune their ears to what they see and hear. More often than not, the students do not even need my prompting. They get the point as soon as we embark on the mission field.

At Barth House we sought to do both local and international missions. In the local missions, soup kitchens, Habitat for Humanity, Helping-Hand, tutoring, and shelter for the homeless, are some of the areas we participated. In the international missions, we made several trips to Kenya. In May 2006, we made one mission trip to Kenya, where we took medical supplies for a health center in Matharite Village in Central Kenya. This is an area where the nearest hospital is forty kilometers away. Ambulances are unknown here. The roads are dirt and when it rains the car has to be pushed a long way to get to the nearest gravel or tarmac road.

Living in this area, and as the only person privileged to own a car, I cannot recount how many times I was awakened in the middle of the night to take a patient to the hospital. Sometimes it was a mother whose labor pains had suddenly come and now realized she couldn't wait until daybreak. I would dress up and join the two or three women accompanying the patient. Sometimes it was not uncommon to have the patient ask for an emergency stop. The baby couldn't wait. The women would ask me to pull over, and they would deliver the baby. Sometimes these good ladies asked me to turn back and take the mother and baby home. Other times they asked that we proceed to the hospital for more specialized care for the mother and baby.

I recall with sadness several cases where things just went terribly wrong. In one case a neighboring mother had delivered her baby at home. She was bleeding profusely. The woman's husband had left the village to work in the city to provide for the family. The family could not get in touch with him in good time. Cell phones were not available then. I was called by the neighbors to take the patient to the hospital. Unfortunately it was too late. The woman regrettably died of complications. At such times, I couldn't help thinking that that was a death which should not have happened. All that was needed was for a woman like this to have proper prenatal care. All she needed was a medical assistant or qualified midwife during her delivery. But this is an area where prenatal care was rare, since pregnant mothers had to travel long distances to the nearest clinic.

In another case, the father of a good elementary school classmate of mine was sick at home. Neither of his two sons was at home. They were both in the city working and the man's wife was helpless. It is not uncommon for folks in the village to stay sick in bed even though they well know they are sick and needed to be hospitalized. Sometimes folks like these have mistrust for doctors. Others do not have the money to hire a vehicle to take them to the hospital. Others simply do not have enough money for medical services. So they would choose to stay in bed sick and hoping that they would get better.

I had come home from my parish and was asked to take the man to the hospital. I recall talking with him and asking him what was the matter with him as we put him in the back seat of my Datsun station wagon. He told me that he had a cold. Now I think that the man had pneumonia. I started the car to take the patient to the hospital accompanied by two men who were supporting him. We had hardly gone more than one mile when one of the men asked me to stop. The patient had died. It was unbelievable to me. I turned round and took the body home where we prepared for his burial. That was yet another of many deaths that never should have happened.

So for me to participate and to actually see the construction of a health center in the community where I grew up was a dream come true. To show up with a group of ten missionaries bearing medical supplies ranging from bandages, stethoscopes, microscopes, syringes, etcetera, was a time of great celebration. For my college students, this was an eye-opening experience. They have always had doctor's appointments whenever they needed to see one. Their parents took them to the shot nurse for their immunizations. For them to see the whole village come to welcome us with songs, dance and speeches of thankfulness for generosity accorded them was a lasting legacy. For me to go back to this community after three months and see the health center in full operation with mothers and children and other patients getting the medical help they needed was a great joy. To see patients coming from all over the region for laboratory tests was a most gratifying experience to me.

Leaving Matharite Village, the mission team went to Juja Farm, another location in Central Kenya, where we were to work for one week with the local community on an irrigation project. Digging trenches in the scorching sun alongside the local people and gluing the PVC pipes together to provide water to these people, was an experience like no other. The local people worked hard with contagious smiles on their faces, grateful that caring people had come from abroad to give them a hand. The team often spiced the task with work and praise songs, giving glory to God for the blessings they had received or reviving their spirits to continue working. A short break to either chew sugar cane or take a cup of *uji* (porridge) or water came as a most welcome respite to the yet unbroken students. The students get to learn that happiness is not contingent on material possessions. They get to see a people who have very little material wealth, but who are enormously grateful for the little they have. Their spirit of sharing their meager resources and their hard work will forever be embedded in the minds of these students.

Community Service

Mission does not necessarily have to be done abroad. There is a whole lot that needs to be done locally. Some of our local community services included working in the soup kitchens. More than a Meal program at Grace/St. Luke's is a good example. We buy the food, in this case twelve trays of lasagna and an equal number of salad bags and cakes, for dessert. The Church kitchen at Grace/St. Luke's is commercial and, therefore, comes in very handy for this kind of project. In addition, this project has other volunteers. This means that we are not alone to do it. So we team up with others. We cook the food, set the tables, seat the guests and serve them. We serve them seconds and dessert. Each one of them has enough to eat.

Sometimes, after we have served all the guests, we each take a plate and sit with the guests and engage them in conversation. For me, this is the most important aspect of this ministry. We get to relate to the guests. We hear their stories. Some of these guests are very bright people with a lot of experience. In talking with them, one hears how they made bad choices, which led them to alcoholism or drug addiction or jail. They lost their jobs and nobody is able to trust them again to give them another job. One of the persons I talked with had been arrested more than fifteen times! Yet here was a person consumed with pride and unable to grasp the reality of his situation. I made an appointment to see him in my office. I have to confess that after two meetings, I realized that his case was more than I could handle.

Other cases are less complicated than that. These are persons who simply are not able to make ends meet and need a meal for the day. They are most grateful to have a hot, home-cooked meal. Our college students encounter these persons and the experience is more meaningful than a lecture given in class on hunger and homelessness in the city. Sometimes, on going back to Barth House, we would talk about our project and how it impacted on us. It was always very interesting to hear student encounters.

Food Distribution

Another way of feeding the hungry is the distribution of food. In one of those projects we joined a larger group of other volunteers at the Fairgrounds in Memphis to distribute food to the hungry. The food was donated and brought to the site by the "Convoy of Hope," an organization committed to feeding the hungry in this country. Our task was to bag and distribute the food to hundreds of people who had lined up to get the food. As we teamed together on this project, again the impact was tremendous. One gets a real sense of hunger in the city. One gets to see how thankful people are to be able to get a bag of groceries. This saves them a trip to the local grocery store and of course, much needed cash. The cash saved will enable them to buy other necessities. But the experience also helps our students to be more thankful for the blessings of daily food that God gives us. The experience is a lasting legacy.

Habitat for Humanity

The basic human needs include food and shelter. Having a shelter for one and his/her family is a right of every human being, especially the people of this great country. The American dream includes the opportunity to own a home. Unfortunately, there are many people in this great country - the land of opportunity- that still do not have a shelter. There are many homeless persons in Memphis. This is not unique to Memphis, but is a common problem in most large cities.

Some people lose their homes because of a series of factors. One loses a job and is consequently unable to keep up with the mortgage payment. His/her home is repossessed. Another one may have faced a crippling medical bill that led from one thing to another. Before long, the person and his/her family were rendered homeless. Other persons are homeless because of their own wrong choices. Either way, homelessness takes away human dignity. Without a home, one is unable to live a decent life, get a job, give an address to a prospective employer, or even allow one to maintain the basics of personal hygiene. So, providing a home is not only the good thing to do for Christians, it is the logical thing to do for citizens of a city like Memphis.

Habitat for Humanity is an appropriate community project for students. It involves joining hands with others in doing the basic building chores such as hammering nails, painting, installing floors, and cleaning, among others. It is a team effort. Working together gives students the opportunity to meet other caring members of the community: church leaders, philanthropists, activists and even local politicians. It bonds them as a team.

When the project is finally completed and the working crew comes together for the dedication ceremony of the new home, the feeling is most fulfilling. But what is even more fulfilling is to see the owner of the new home take the keys and open her/his house for the first time. Sometimes this takes place with tears of joy streaming down his/her cheeks. There is no greater lesson for our students than to participate and witness this kind of experience. It gives them an opportunity to do something for someone else and to witness the transforming power of a good deed.

Gulu Walk

Other community projects are not directly related to our immediate community, but rather are a witness to the reality of the global village we live in. One such project is the Gulu Walk. Gulu is a district in the northern part of Uganda. In this area child soldiers were literally stolen from their families and drafted in the army. Some of these children were as young as 12-16 years when they were forced into the training camps away from their families. Having received the basics of using a gun, the child soldiers are armed with AK-47s and forced to kill, sometimes even members of their own families. To avoid the drafting, some of the children run away walking long distances in the night with hardly anything to eat.

The Gulu Walk is therefore an activists' movement to raise the consciousness of the global community to the evils of war especially when children are involved. But it is also a chance to raise funds to be used for the purposes of stopping this war and for helping those children who managed to find their way into refugee camps. We organized a group of students to participate in the Gulu Walk. Wearing wrist bands, hats and T-shirts, we joined other participants for the walk. We walked in Downtown Memphis, with the police directing traffic. An address at the end of the walk by the organizers thanked the walkers, but also asked them to keep the fire of the walk going.

Participation in this kind of event leads our students to appreciate that we are indeed a global community. They learn to appreciate that we are in one boat, sharing one destiny. They appreciate that what happens in one corner of this global village has consequences and effects in another and, indeed, all parts of this village. We all go home from the walk with a feeling of satisfaction that perhaps we have made a difference in the lives of children in a distant land in East Africa

Tutoring

As part of our student community outreach, a group of Barth House students regularly participated in the tutoring program in the local areas. One of these students recruited me into this program. The United Methodist Church at the corner of Tillman and Walnut Grove, is one of these centers. Some of the kids who came to this center were from immigrant families. In this particular center, there were many kids from the Sudanese immigrants living in Memphis. For these children, English is a second language. They certainly need all the help they can get to go through their homework. The program coordinator, herself a graduate of the University of Memphis, assigned tutors to help several kids, with their English, Mathematics and other kinds of homework. The fact that English is a second language does not mean that these kids are stupid. On the contrary, most of them are smart kids who know clearly that their future relies on their getting an education. Unlike many American students, who often take life for granted, these are hard-working kids who are willing to receive all the help they can get to reach their goals.

It was most reassuring to work with these kids, helping them through their homework. I often left the center with a sense of satisfaction that I had helped a child prepare for the next day with his/her teacher. One could see the deep appreciation in the radiant smiles on the faces of these children. It is this kind of satisfaction that brought volunteer tutors back again and again. The student tutors not only helped the children but also became their role models, motivating them to greater academic achievements. But as with every community or mission work, it always works both ways. In helping others, we help ourselves. This is true with the tutoring program. It gives the college students a sense of purpose and energizes them in their own academic pursuits. In seeking to change the lives of others, their own lives are changed for the better.

Summer Sunday Night Movie Program

Over summer, most college students go away to be with their parents, work or travel abroad. However, there are other students who stay in school for summer classes and other school programs. Other students are local and need not go away. For these students, the summer movie program comes in handy. We plan a series of topical movies that students like to see and discuss. The program begins with a pizza or homemade meal. This is followed by showing the movie and discussion. Some of the movies we screened include: *The Green Mile, Dead Men Walking, A Day Without a Mexican, The Power of One, The Shawshank Redemption, The Second Chance*, to name a few. These are great movies with contemporary ethical, justice, political and social issues to discuss. The forum presents a great opportunity for fellowship, teachable moments and learning. The program concludes with Compline at around 8:30 - 9:00 P.M. By the time summer is over, the summer Sunday night movie group easily transitions into the regular semester programs.

Choir

Some of the most effective college ministry programs are those that are student-initiated and directed. The role of the college chaplain in this case is to facilitate, support, encourage and, wherever possible, participate alongside the students. One of these programs at the University of Memphis was the Barth House choir. The motto of our choir was, "Make a joyful noise to the Lord." Ben Smith, our choir director, was a law student who had also graduated as music major for his bachelor's degree. He was actively involved in our worship and Bible study programs. In his second year he approached me with the idea of having a choir for our chaplaincy. I embraced the idea and made the announcement to the community. We gathered a group of students and adult participants to form the choir. True to our motto, one did not have to be musically literate to become a member.

Pitfalls

Some sang just for the joy of singing. I happen to fall into this category. Others, like my organist, were more professional. Sam, a doctoral student in the School of Music, and later his wife, were great participants of the Barth House choir.

Ben chose very attractive and easy-to-sing songs. I put together a small budget that enabled us to purchase the music, T-shirts for choir members and some DVDs. Ben brought his violin, keyboard and DVD player. Our organist, also a member of the student choir, played the organ. The Barth House choir met for practice every Sunday for two hours before the 6:00 P.M worship service. The choir enhanced our worship and attracted other students who came to hear us sing. The mission of the choir was expanded to comprise an outreach for college ministry. We undertook to sing Christmas carols and Easter hymns for residents at Trezevant Manor, a local nursing home. We coordinated with the nursing home staff, who gathered the residents in the hall for us. It was most fulfilling to see the residents sing along with us, nodding their heads and clapping for us after every hymn. A short intermission allowed us to introduce ourselves and read the gospel lesson for the season for the residents and to wish them a "Merry Christmas" or "Happy Easter." The residents greatly appreciated these visits.

The Barth House choir also made a few visits to the local parishes where we sang one or two selections. Twice we sang in the Diocesan Convention, where we invited delegates to join us in one or two choruses. These were great opportunities for promoting college ministry. These visits were much appreciated and paid dividends as more and more people in the Diocese came to know what was happening in college ministry.

Recruitment

Getting college students to come through the doors of religious houses is the goal, but also the nightmare of every college chaplain. There is no one way of recruiting students to college chaplaincy. What may have worked last year may not necessarily work this year. The college chaplain must constantly vary his/her methods. Here are some suggestions that have been proven to work.

Our freshmen orientation program in the Religious Life Staff alongside other student organizations under the Office of the Dean of Students is described above and need not be repeated here. This was the most effective program of reaching out to students in a public university. As already pointed out, at the end of each session, the cards were sorted out and each denominational representative given theirs. It was an open secret that the Baptists got the lion's share of the freshmen recruitment cards. I still recall one session when I got only two cards signed by students who identified themselves as Episcopalians. My Baptist colleague had received one hundred and fifty cards in this session. Comforting me, my colleague said. "Do not take it personally, Samson; being a Baptist in the South is a tradition." From then on I was contented to get anywhere from ten to twenty cards for a whole season of freshmen orientation.

Pitfalls

I used these cards to write directly to the students, by mail or email or addresses given on the card, inviting them to our Episcopal/Anglican programs. The letter always made a personal appeal to the freshmen. We would normally get several students to join us in our programs from these endeavors.

At CBU, where denominational preference is checked out by students in their admission forms, the Catholic chaplains generously shared this information with us, allowing us to write directly to the Episcopal students, inviting them to our programs. I am particularly most grateful to Sister Delores and Brother Rob who were most supportive to me in this ministry. These colleagues treated me with respect. Brother Rob, the last chaplain I worked with at CBU, even had my picture posted with his on the CBU College Ministry website. Working together, we came to realize that it is not a matter of competition but complementing what others are doing. This becomes evident when one realizes that even in a denominationally affiliated college such as CBU, only 35% of the students are Roman Catholics in any given year. All the rest come from other denominations. They, too, need spiritual guidance.

At Rhodes College, a students' fair at the beginning of the fall semester was our primary forum for recruiting Episcopal students. A promotional table, complete with flyers and sign up-sheets, was provided. The Episcopal student leadership was most helpful in this regard. Students would visit each table and sign up for organizations of their preference. Normally the Episcopal student population would be about 150 students, out of a total of 1,500 students. This translates into 10%, a very high number for a college that is non-Episcopal in its affiliation. At one such students' fair, we got anywhere from 20-30 students to sign up to participate in our Episcopal activities. This left out over one hundred other Episcopal students out there. Unfortunately, unlike CBU, Rhodes College was not as helpful in sharing their student information. They cited student confidentiality. The best they would do for us was to take our flyers and give them to the college chaplain's office, who would, in turn, have a work study student distribute them to the Episcopal students' mail boxes. Sometimes we followed the student fair recruitment with promotional tables at the cafeteria. This provided an opportunity to meet and talk with more students on their way to and from the cafeteria.

The Daily Helmsman

The Daily Helmsman is the campus weekly paper at the University of Memphis. The publication runs throughout the academic year except in the summer and other university breaks. Twice each summer, the *Daily Helmsman*, published two large issues that went out to all the incoming freshmen and their parents, reaching 6,000 to 8,000 students. In these special issues we advertised our fall programs, open house, or any other eye-catching event that we had planned. As registered student organizations, each religious life house qualified for students' activity funds for up to 400 dollars per semester. We used these funds to pay for our advertisements in the two special issues. In addition, the weekly issue of *the Daily Helmsman* used to carry a column entitled "U of M this week." We used this column to advertise our weekly programs without any charge. This was a good way of reminding students about the programs we offered at Barth House.

The Living Church

The Living Church, an Episcopal Church magazine, designates some of its August and September issues to college ministry. The magazine is widely read in the Episcopal Church. We advertised our college ministry programs in these summer issues of the *Living Church*. This was particularly helpful to the out-of-state students and parents looking for college ministry. It was not uncommon to receive a call from a parent who may have read about our programs in the *Living Church* magazine. Such a parent would be anxious to have his/her child participate in college ministry. The parent would kindly give us the name of his/her child, which enabled us to write a more personal note to the student or simply call to invite him/her to our programs. Advertising in the *Living Church* was more expensive, but it was money well spent in promoting our programs and ensuring that every student looking for college ministry could easily find us.

Letters to Parish Rectors and Youth Directors

College ministry is, to some extent, also an extension of youth ministry from the parishes. It is, therefore, logical that the college chaplain gets into some liaison with the diocesan and parish youth directors and the local parish priests. One way of doing this is by writing letters to these youth workers as early as the beginning of summer, when most college admissions have already taken place. The purpose of the letter is to ask these youth directors to give the chaplain the names and contacts of all those young adults going to college from their parishes. The letter also seeks to impress the youth directors that what the college chaplain is doing is an extension of what they do with the young adults in the EYC and other youth forums.

Some of the students whose names the college chaplain gets may not be attending college where the chaplain is located. But through networking, the chaplain is able to contact colleagues in other campuses where these students will be going to school. This is a shared ministry and networking is essential to its success.

Parent Contacts

Another most effective way of recruitment is getting names of college freshmen directly from their parents. This takes place when the college chaplain speaks in the local parishes or encounters parents in diocesan events where he/she makes an appeal for this contact. Most parents are anxious to have their college-bound children well placed in school and their spiritual welfare taken care of. They are most helpful in working with college chaplains. This requires trust. So the more the college chaplain is exposed to parents and youth leaders in the diocese, the easier it becomes for this kind of networking to take place.

Other parents, especially those from out of town, check out the college chaplaincy from the website and make a point of calling the chaplain, directly giving him/her the name of their child in college. This information is most helpful. It allows the chaplain to contact the students, inviting them to the college ministry programs. In some cases, the parents may not want their children to know that they have given their names to the college chaplain. The chaplain must respect this confidentiality in approaching particular students. It must never be forgotten that freshmen, in particular, are, for the first time, seeking to establish their own independence from their parents. Any attempt for parents to appear to control them in college is most likely to be resisted and to have a negative impact.

Resident Assistants

Resident Assistants are very resourceful people in doing college ministry in residential settings. These are the people who are with the students on a day-to-day basis in the dorms. Part of their job description is for RAs to organize monthly dorm activities for their residents. Some of these activities may be religious in nature. They may be ethical, racial, political or relational discussions. College chaplains are resourceful and available to the RAs as speakers in these types of forums.

The Religious Life Staff at the University of Memphis hosts RA luncheons at the beginning of every fall semester. The purpose of these luncheons is to allow RAs to meet the college chaplains from the various religious houses and to know that they are available to work with them. So the luncheon includes fellowship, but also several workshops on topics of interest to the college students' life. The forums also give each college chaplain the opportunity to introduce themselves and their programs in their particular religious houses. The program works well. The next time the chaplain makes a dorm visit or is invited to speak on a topic in the student resident life he/she is no longer a stranger.

RAs also get the contacts of the college chaplains. These contacts are resourceful in the event that an RA has an emergency that may require the intervention of a college chaplain. To be sure, not every type of student conflict may be appropriate to be handled by a college chaplain. The university has its own machinery. However, this machinery does not preclude the college chaplains.

Dorm Postings

In seeking to promote our programs, we make every effort to post our flyers in campus bulletins, dorm hallways, the student center or any other place designated for such postings. The RAs are most helpful in this regard. The Office of Resident Life at the University of Memphis readily works with college chaplains. Of course not every flyer will be posted in the dorm hallways. The Office of Resident Life approves the flyers that go on their bulletin boards. They ask that we send them the number of flyers

Pitfalls

we wish to post. The office approves and stamps them for us and gives them to the RAs to post in their dorms for us. This networking is most helpful to the college chaplain. This same arrangement applies at CBU and Rhodes College.

All this goes to show that it is important for college chaplains to see themselves as part of the college administration in seeking to do their work. When that happens, chaplains find their work become much easier. It is no longer like fighting city hall, but rendering much needed service to city hall. The ministry becomes mutually beneficial. It's all geared to helping the students be better persons, assist in their retention and better equip them for their academic challenges. This does not mean that college chaplains will not use their prophetic voice when necessary, to advocate for issues of concern to students. The college chaplain enjoys a unique independence that allows him/her to adequately play these two roles.

Promotional Tables

This involves setting up tables at the Student Center with our house merchandise. The merchandise may include, flyers, key chains, pens, cookies, and blow pops. To do this, the Director of the University Student Center requires chaplains to reserve a date and time when they wish to do their promotion. We would choose a time when most students were coming from class or going to lunch or generally when student traffic is heaviest at the Center. Students will normally freely stop by to pick a flyer or ask about our programs. We would take the chance to tell them where on the campus we are located and what our programs are. We would invite them to come and check us out. Giving a key chain or a pen with the name of our religious life house and contact is an added benefit to this program. It allows the students to contact us after some time or when they need us. Two or three such promotions per semester are enough for this purpose. This approach enables us to go where the students are and not just wait for them to come and look for us. Sometimes this works great. Other times it may not work as well. One may never know until they try!

Direct Flyer Handout

This method involves direct handouts to the students. All it requires is for us to time when the students come out from classes or are on their way to class from their dorms. We give them our program handouts and invite them to come to our programs. The handout is an opportunity for us to draw the students' attention to our existence and what we have to offer. In the spring of 2007, we handed out over two thousand flyers. It gives us an opportunity to talk directly to the students. Sometimes, a student is not in a big hurry and stops to inquire more about our programs. Some students will come to check us out from the contact information on the flyer we have given them. When that happens, the flyer has had its desired effect.

There is no doubt Episcopalians are shy about using these types of aggressive methods of advertising our presence and programs. But just walk around in the malls or downtown areas and this is what one finds. If it works for others, we should not cling to the old notion that "we don't do it that way." The question is, "Does it work?" To know the answer to this question, go ahead and try it.

Promotional Tent

The first two to three weeks of the fall semester are crucial to college ministry. Students are shopping around for classes and programs they wish to try in the year. Chances are that if we get a student to participate in our programs in these two to three weeks, we most likely will keep them for the year. The opposite is true. If we do not get a student during these first few weeks, chances are that their time and priorities will be focused elsewhere. To ensure that we have marketed ourselves properly, we would pitch a promotional tent outside Barth House, which is conspicuously located on the direct path of students coming and going to class from the Richardson Towers. We would furnish the tent with a table, a music player, flyers, sign-up sheets and, of course, cookies and pink lemonade, to attract the students. Pink lemonade was the official Barth House drink. The lemonade is irresistible to students on a hot summer day, when everybody tends to perspire a lot.

The promotional tent gave us an opportunity to meet and talk with students. We would tell them about our ongoing or up-coming programs. Those interested in becoming members of Barth House would sign up and give us their contact information. This would enable

The Rev. Dr. Samson N. Gitau

us to follow-up with them by placing them in our regular weekly email bulletin, informing them of our ongoing programs. We would do the tent program two to three days a week for three weeks.

Promotional tent

Open House

Even with all the promotions and advertising, it never failed to surprise me to hear how many students said that they were unaware of religious life houses, in general, and Barth House, in particular. As adjunct professor of religion, I would introduce myself to my classes and tell them who I was and that my primary job was college chaplain. I would then ask how many of them were involved in college ministry. I would be lucky if I got one or two students to raise up their hands. I would also be

Pitfalls

equally lucky if I heard one student who said that they knew where Barth House was located and the programs we offered there. It is true that people see what they want to see. My discovery made me all the more determined to market our programs even more and never to take for granted that every student was aware that we existed and that we had programs to offer.

One good way to begin the semester is to have an open house during the first or second weekend of the fall semester. Publicity is important for the success of an open house. Placing flyers in dorm halls, and dining rooms, advertisements in the school paper, yard signs, and emails are some of the ways to promote this event. A good cookout is equally essential. Some times at Barth House we enlisted the help of our college ministry friends from the local parishes, such as Cursillistas, and lovers of college ministry. Our friends from St. John's Episcopal Church and Cursillo members from St. George's and St. Andrew's, were right on board when I asked them to come and help us. We would plan a good menu for the occasion. Barbecue, hamburgers, hot dogs, chips, cake and brownies are all part of the mix. Students love to eat. As the saying goes "where there is food, people will congregate." This is more so with college students.

Outside help freed me from getting tied to the food details and, instead, allowed me to concentrate on the service preceding the meal with enough time to welcome the students to the open house and tell them about our programs. A strong local support from local parishes translates into a strong college ministry even for a free-standing college ministry model.

The Rev. Dr. Samson N. Gitau

Attractive Programs

College ministry is like a restaurant. Have the right kind of food, parking and the right price and customers will come. Attractive programs will attract students. The challenge is to know what program is right for students at any given time. The chaplain must interact with students. He/she must involve them in brainstorming at the beginning of every year to know which programs are desirable to the students. Get the students to own the programs. It's an ongoing process. Eventually, the chaplain hits a home run. But even hitting a home run in one inning does not guarantee hitting another one in the second or third or even ninth inning. The chaplain just has to keep working hard and never become complacent. He/she must keep working and improving on the signature programs while at the same time devising new ones. The Episcopal worship is attractive to some students, faculty and staff alike. At the U of M one looking for liturgical worship knew that he could get it at Barth House. The same with Bible study.

Food

The metaphor of college ministry as a restaurant is not accidental. Food is a main draw to college students. Students want something different from what they eat in the campus dining halls. They are looking for ways and means of saving a few bucks. College programming must have a food budget. Throughout my ten years of college ministry at Barth House, I was on the whole blessed to have a good food budget. I was also blessed to

Pitfalls

have assistants whose responsibility included shopping and preparing meals for Wednesday lunch and Sunday dinner after services.

At Rhodes College, CBU and LeMoyne-Owen College, occasional pizza was warmly welcomed by the students. I regularly packaged cookies and brownies, apples and lemonade in these visits and services outside Barth House. Sometimes, we went out to a local restaurant of the students' choice for a meal. Again, the primary purpose for this food is to facilitate a forum for student conversation and bonding over a meal or snacks. Just as breaking bread together reminds us that we are one body, eating together bonds college students. It provides a relaxed atmosphere for a conversation or simply for students to catch up with one another. As much as possible, we celebrated students' birthdays. It's always special for a student-participant to have the rest of the community remember his/her birthday and to have a cake and a card for the occasion. The chaplaincy is the students' family.

Thanksgiving

One of our signature meals at Barth House throughout the years of my college ministry was the pre-Thanksgiving dinner. We always held this dinner the Sunday before Thanksgiving. This allowed us to celebrate the holidays before most students left campus to go home for Thanksgiving with their families. It also gave us a chance to fellowship with the international students, who often did not have anywhere to go during these holidays.

The dinner gave international students the chance to celebrate in this all inclusive American holiday.

For the purpose of this meal, we bought the biggest turkey in the grocery store. Though I, myself, did not grow up cooking and eating turkey in Kenya, I have over the years become a self-made expert in cooking turkey. Able students brought such trimmings as they were able to bring, while we cooked the other dishes. Of course, the meal was preceded by a service of thanksgiving where I invited students to share their stories about the things for which they were thankful. This is an opportunity to reflect upon those things that we have in life but which we often take for granted: the opportunity to be in college, our parents and friends, good health, our daily bread, the gift of one another, those men and women who support us in college ministry. My favorite chorus for this occasion is: "Count your blessings one by one." As we begin to count our blessings, each one of us finds that there are many things for which we should be most grateful. Even those of us who may be facing hardships, say, in our academic pursuit, tuition, or troubled relationships, begin to appreciate our glasses as half full rather than half empty. Gathering around the altar for Holy Eucharist and thereafter, at the dining table for the meal sealed and affirmed these testimonies from all of us.

Retreats

Regular retreats are effective ways and means of developing a strong college ministry leadership and fellowship. This is especially crucial at the beginning of the fall semester when another bunch of new students have joined the college ministry community. Timing and planning are essential to a successful college ministry retreat. Fall break may be one opening for this kind of program. The new students will have had a couple of months in college. The continuing students will have casually met the new students in the weekly programs. Spring break may be another consideration. This time may present a window when students may not be overwhelmed with assignments.

It is important to balance the program between serious discussion and leisure. The retreat is a time for the students to meet and bond with one another. It is also a time to reflect on the ongoing programs - what is working, what is not working and why. It is a time for brainstorming on what the students would like to see offered by way of programs for their college ministry. It is also a time to grow spiritually. A good Bible study and prayer are good ways to begin the day in the retreat. The retreat is also a time for leadership recruitment and development. The chaplain gets to observe and encourage the talents of the students participating in the retreat. The retreat is also a time of fun. Ideal games, both indoors and outdoors, that involve most students are most helpful. The games create team spirit among the students. The retreat is also a time to cook and eat together. A well-planned menu will do some magic in this program.

Talents Sunday

One of our practices in college ministry was to designate one Sunday as, "Talent Sunday." Students get to share their diverse talents in such areas as: singing, poetry, testimony and skits. Several times on these talent Sundays I had one of the students give a homily. Talent Sunday had the tremendous effect of bringing out the best in each student-participant. As is true to the whole body of Christ, students are endowed with a wide variety of talents. Given the opportunity to share, students bring out the best in themselves.

Student Invitations

Statistics show that eighty percent of the people who join a new church, above everything else, do so because somebody cared enough to invite them to go to church with them. College ministry is no exception to this trend. Students are the best ambassadors for college ministry. We encourage our students to bring their friends to our programs. It works. These may be dorm roommates or friends made in class or in other college forums. In other cases, college ministry is a forum for dates, worship or community service. If young adults are going on a date, I cannot think of a better and safer place for them to do so than in college ministry programs. Successful college ministry programs are student-engaging. Like any other organization, students will readily support a program in which they have a sense of ownership.

Shrove Tuesday

By now it should be evident that any successful college ministry requires the involvement of faculty and staff in

Pitfalls

one way or another. One of the most successful faculty/staff programs we had at Barth House was the Shrove Tuesday luncheon. Shrove Tuesday is the day before Ash Wednesday that marks the beginning of the Lenten Season. It is traditional for Christians, Episcopalians in particular, to indulge in pancakes and sausages before they began the Lenten Season, when they may give up some luxuries. On Shrove Tuesday, also known as Fat Tuesday, one may stuff him/herself with food without a feeling of guilt. We used this occasion to invite faculty and staff from our four colleges to join us for the luncheon. Aware of the different schedules for these busy people, we organized the luncheon to run from 11:00 A.M. to 2:00 P.M. We were sensitive to cook a soup in lieu of pancakes and sausages for most of our healthy-conscious guests. The luncheon was an occasion for faculty and staff to meet and fellowship with one another and to familiarize themselves with our programs. We invited them to see how they could continue participating in these programs or helping us to draw the attention of their students to our programs.

Faculty Support

Doing college ministry programs in the four colleges, I deliberately sought to meet the Episcopal faculty and staff. I introduced myself and invited them to participate in our programs. I discovered that there are many Episcopalians working in these colleges as faculty and administrators. Dr. Nelson of the political science department at Rhodes was gracious enough to organize an afternoon tea for our Rhodes College students. Dr. Moore of the English department at LeMoyne-Owen College, was helpful in showing me my way around college. Ms. Dorothy Brownyard in the admissions office at Rhodes was always most resourceful with student contacts. Ms. Noel Schwartz, registrar at the U of M was of tremendous support in many ways. Dr. Mary Cargill of CBU was a great supporter and participant in our programs. Dr. Susan Darnell, acting dean of University College at the U of M was equally supportive. Dr. Lavonnie Perry-Claybon, was always there for us at Barth House as student adviser for many years. Mr. Curt Guenther in the administration at the U of M was resourceful in providing data when we needed it. So was Rebecca Lomann in the international students' immigration office at the U of M. Mr. Alan Bray of the School of Business Administration at the U of M spent many hours helping us set up the Barth House website and linking it with the other three colleges. The list of Episcopal faculty and staff in these colleges could go on and on. Their help in doing college ministry was invaluable. Each one of them was resourceful in our ministry. I did not hesitate to solicit their help when I needed it.

The wide variety of programs highlighted in this chapter, some regular, others occasional, demonstrates the type of thriving college ministry we had at Barth House at the U of M and in the other colleges we served. We never had a shortage of programs. However, it is always best to hear it from the horse's mouth. Chapter six will, therefore, present some of the student voices and what these college ministry programs meant to them.

Chapter Six

Student Voices

> *"You yourselves are our letter of recommendation, written on your hearts to be known and read by all men; and you show that you are a letter from Christ delivered by us, written not in ink but with the Spirit of the living God not on tablets of stone but on tablets of human hearts"* (2 Cor. 3:2-3)

It is 9.00 P.M; I am relaxing after dinner with my family. The telephone rings. "Fr. Samson, this is Cecilia, I am sorry to call you at home, but one of my friends has a very big problem. She is suicidal. Can you please talk to her?" "Sure," I answer, even before I know the magnitude of the problem. "When would you and your friend like to come see me?" I asked. "Can she come see you tomorrow morning?" Cecilia asked. "Certainly, I will be glad to talk to her after Morning Prayer at 8:00 A.M." "Ok, I will not be able to come with her, but one of our mutual friends, will accompany her to your office tomorrow morning." Cecilia says.

The next day, even before Morning Prayer was over, I saw two ladies enter the library. We finish Morning Prayer at 8:30 A.M. and I invite my two guests to my office. Sure enough, Cecilia's friend is in very bad shape. Her face looks grim and it is obvious she has been crying and may not have had much sleep either. I talk with her and find out that she has problems with her oriental parents always telling her what to do and what not to do, in spite of the fact that Sue (not her real name) is over 20 years old. Sue commutes from home where she lives with her parents. It becomes evident that here is a case of clash of cultures. Sue's oriental culture expects her to obey her parents without exception. It is disrespectful to answer back your superiors, especially when they are your parents. But now Sue has been raised in the American culture with its excessive child freedom and where most children have no sense of obligation to participate in family chores, other than eat and entertain themselves on TV and video games. Sue is not exactly a saint herself. She has abused drugs and alcohol too. Half way through our conversation Sue becomes sick and is about to throw up. Her friend rushes her to the bathroom where she throws up and calms down. They come back. We finish the conversation and I ask Sue if I could pray with her and her friend. We bow in prayer and I pray for Sue's healing. Sue thanks me profusely and says that she already feels better. In our conversation I had managed to persuade Sue that it was of no purpose to commit suicide. I had also managed to convince her to see her doctor. One week later, I received the following note from Cecilia:

"Dear Fr. Samson,

I cannot thank you enough for talking to Sue last week. I do apologize for calling you @ home. Sue has been doing much better. She's going to see a doctor regularly.

Please continue to pray for her. Thank you so much for everything."

Peace, O (using her nick name).

This is an example of some of the situations that college ministers have to contend with. It's being there for students at the time of need. It's assuring students that life has meaning beyond apparent failures and meaninglessness.

I recently received an email signed by a former Rhodes College student who came to our Episcopal students' programs. At first, I honestly couldn't put a face to the name signed in the email. But the content of this email made my day. This is what it said:

Dear Samson,

"I was having a discussion on faith earlier today, and when speaking of individuals who had made an impact in my life, your name dropped suddenly into the conversation. When I first came to know you and your family while I was at Rhodes several years back, I had been separated from my beliefs for so long that I felt a certain level of guilt at even being in your presence in the chapel at Rhodes. It wasn't because of my life or my choices--surprisingly enough, I managed on many levels to stay on the "right" path--relatively speaking--- but because I felt I had no place being there when I knew to what level I did not believe--- your kindness and faith were a light when I had none, and I never really had the opportunity to convey that to you while I was still living in Memphis....."

(Courtney, Rhodes College)

This student had graduated two years before sending this email. Apparently the impact made on her in college ministry had left a lasting imprint in her life. It is easy for college ministers to underestimate the impact we have on our students by simply living our Christian lives the way God calls us to do and by doing with grace, what God calls us to do. Our presence on campus is most reassuring. It is like walking down the streets in downtown and seeing some police presence around the corner. Whereas one may not necessarily need their services, it is reassuring to know that they are available should one have a need for them. College students readily turn to college ministers when the need arises.

My administrative assistant and I recently hosted a promotional table at the student center. It was a Monday morning. We handed out flyers to those who cared to stop by. One of those who stopped by was a young man known as W. We took W through the various programs listed in our flyer. One of these programs was Morning Prayer. This is not one of the most popular programs especially because we do it early before classes begin. Most students are either sleepily walking to class or looking for breakfast before classes began. But W came to Morning Prayer in my chapel the following day. He continued coming. He had found a way to begin his day in school.

At the end of the week W had to work in the dorm where he tutored other students, but before our Sunday service began at 6:00 P.M., W came to the chapel. He asked me to pray with him before he went to work. He greatly regretted being unable to attend the evening service, but he wanted me to know how energized he

Pitfalls

had become after attending Morning Prayer with us all week. He was especially grateful that I had asked him to read one of the lessons for the day. The assignment made him feel included. He said that he had found a new sense of purpose in his life.

Whether it is in parish ministry, classroom, or even a company setting, most people appreciate feedback. This is more so with positive feedback. Feedback helps us gauge whether or not we are on the right track. I do not mean the kind of feedback parishioners give to their ministers at the exit door, almost as an obligatory duty to the effect that "I enjoyed the sermon," or "the sermon was great," but when asked what they particularly liked or how it impacted their own lives, they would be hard pressed to do so. I am referring to genuine feedback where the giver can clearly point out how they have been impacted. This kind of feedback helps us know the impact we are making upon the lives of the people we serve. In other situations, feedback may help us know the areas in our work and ministry upon which we may need improvement. Here are other samples of student feedbacks in college ministry.

Hey Samson!

I would like to take this time to thank you for everything you have done this year. Not only have you brought Episcopal Mass on campus, but you have helped make faith come alive. Your constant spirit and motivation is an example which I often try to emulate. I believe you have fostered my faith more than you know...I have fallen in love with the liturgy of the Anglican service... Your services, ideals, and actions have influenced me greatly and have helped me develop my faith more than I can say. I look forward to worshiping with you for the rest of my time in Memphis. I am sure that I am one of many students you will transform and nurture during your chaplaincy in Memphis. Thank you, Samson, I appreciate you.

Sincerely,

(Patrick, Rhodes College).

Samson,

Thanks for helping me pray this year. My grades came back and I received 5 As and 1 B (the history class),

Carmen, CBU

Dear Samson,

"I really enjoyed the communion service we had this past Thursday. I am sorry that I have not been able to come earlier. I will be ready to come to the noon service on a regular basis when school starts in the fall." (Brilund, CBU)

Hello Samson,

"How are you? I hope all is going well... I hope you remember me... I have benefited greatly from your help and prayers. My mother is doing great now and all is well... I have even gotten a nice job after I graduated. I think that the prayers helped a great deal. I just wanted to thank you and show my appreciation to you and your faith and help.. you're great."

(Nashwa, CBU)

had become after attending Morning Prayer with us all week. He was especially grateful that I had asked him to read one of the lessons for the day. The assignment made him feel included. He said that he had found a new sense of purpose in his life.

Whether it is in parish ministry, classroom, or even a company setting, most people appreciate feedback. This is more so with positive feedback. Feedback helps us gauge whether or not we are on the right track. I do not mean the kind of feedback parishioners give to their ministers at the exit door, almost as an obligatory duty to the effect that "I enjoyed the sermon," or "the sermon was great," but when asked what they particularly liked or how it impacted their own lives, they would be hard pressed to do so. I am referring to genuine feedback where the giver can clearly point out how they have been impacted. This kind of feedback helps us know the impact we are making upon the lives of the people we serve. In other situations, feedback may help us know the areas in our work and ministry upon which we may need improvement. Here are other samples of student feedbacks in college ministry.

Hey Samson!

I would like to take this time to thank you for everything you have done this year. Not only have you brought Episcopal Mass on campus, but you have helped make faith come alive. Your constant spirit and motivation is an example which I often try to emulate. I believe you have fostered my faith more than you know...I have fallen in love with the liturgy of the Anglican service... Your services, ideals, and actions have influenced me greatly and have helped me develop my faith more than I can say. I look forward to worshiping with you for the rest of my time in Memphis. I am sure that I am one of many students you will transform and nurture during your chaplaincy in Memphis. Thank you, Samson, I appreciate you.

Sincerely,

(Patrick, Rhodes College).

Samson,

Thanks for helping me pray this year. My grades came back and I received 5 As and 1 B (the history class),

Carmen, CBU

Dear Samson,

"I really enjoyed the communion service we had this past Thursday. I am sorry that I have not been able to come earlier. I will be ready to come to the noon service on a regular basis when school starts in the fall." (Brilund, CBU)

Hello Samson,

"How are you? I hope all is going well... I hope you remember me... I have benefited greatly from your help and prayers. My mother is doing great now and all is well... I have even gotten a nice job after I graduated. I think that the prayers helped a great deal. I just wanted to thank you and show my appreciation to you and your faith and help.. you're great."

(Nashwa, CBU)

Pitfalls

This student had graduated from CBU one year prior to writing this email. The email reminded me how she agonized and was unable to concentrate in her studies because of her sick mother. Joining me regularly for Noon Prayer and St. Joseph's Chapel, we prayed for Nashwa's mother and for peace for her to enable her to concentrate in her studies. She made it. Mine was a ministry of presence, encouragement and intercession for her. What else can the college chaplain ask other than to lead a student to fall in love with God and to own his/her faith? This takes place when the chaplain builds rapport with students in worship and fellowship.

Another graduating student from the University of Memphis had this to say:

Dear Fr. Samson,

"Thank you for all the wonderful help you have offered me through school! I shall never forget you and I shall visit often!" (Jennifer, U of M)

Jennifer had been one of our most active students at Barth House. She did her confirmation classes with me and was confirmed at Barth House. Like a proud parent, I saw Jennifer grow in her faith. True to her promise, Jennifer maintained her contact with us at Barth House. She constantly sent seasonal cards assuring us of her prayers in our ministry.

Father Samson,

I just want to thank you for allowing the Lord to use you! God has clearly spoken to me through you many times already, and I look forward to the homily this Sunday when I'm sure He'll use you to speak to me (and everyone else there) again. I also want to thank you for your kindness and generosity. I've felt so welcomed and loved at the Barth house since the first time I met everyone. I pray that the Lord will open up the windows of heaven on you and Lilian and overflow your lives with blessings!

(Abby, U of M)

I should add that Abby met Josh at Barth House. Their romance matured into an engagement and eventually to their marriage. I was honored to solemnize their wedding at the Barth House chapel with their parents and close friends in attendance.

Hey Fr. Samson,

I just wanted to express my gratitude again for the Kenya mission trip. I am so thankful for you and for Barth House in many ways. This year has been such a struggle for me, but Barth House has always been there no matter what. I'm praying to find another job for the upcoming year, so hopefully I will be able to attend more this coming fall. Anyway, thanks again!

(Rachel, U of M).

Mission Trip

Dr. Gitau High School students sing a number for missioners

Following our first mission trip to Kenya in May 2006, I asked each participant to write a paragraph or two on what the trip meant for them and how it had impacted their lives. We had participated in two main projects on this mission trip. We took eight suit cases full of medical supplies for Matharite Village Health Care. We delivered these supplies worth over $5,000.00 to the villagers gathered to welcome us at St. Mark's Anglican Church. Each one of us planted a tree in the Health Center compound to commemorate our trip.

For the next four days, we worked with small farmers at Juja Farm, in an irrigation project, helping them to maximize their farm produce and to serve as a pilot project to other small farmers in the area. We used mattocks and shovels to dig trenches, laid PVC pipes, glued them up and covered the pipes again in readiness for irrigation. The work was hard particularly for American students not used to hard labor and hot sun as experienced in Juja Farm. The students suffered blisters, sunburn and sweat a lot in this project. But at the end of it, it was most fulfilling. Here are some excerpts of what the students said:

"I have learned on this trip that whatever we do in America labor wise is nothing compared with what other people do in other countries. Another thing that I have learned is that the people of Kenya are very hospitable to everyone. They don't care when you visit because they are always glad to see you no matter what time of the day it is. I get out of this trip that no matter what I do, to always be there for someone else." (Christian, SWCC).

"This trip has been very meaningful to me. I have been able to walk into a new country and feel like I never left the old one. I have met people who have become my friends as well as companions here and I feel welcome no matter who I am with. Kenya has shown me what it is like to be truly loved." (Sara, U of M).

"Being in Kenya has affected me in such a way that I can no longer go and just talk about something. I have to DO something about the situation. This is why I WILL NOT be silent anymore. I WILL go back and tell the story of a nation that has great need and much to offer in return. The people of Kenya do not greet you as visitors, but as friends." (Tom, U of M.).

Pitfalls

"The hospitality here is absolutely amazing. Even though they are poor, they still are generous with a smile. My journey has been a rocky road and much time dedication to pain. This trip has taught me to be more giving and forgiving. Family, friends and confidence is what I need to achieve." (Brandon, SWCC).

"I never thought in all my life I would have a chance an opportunity to go to Kenya. I am blessed to have had this opportunity. I have been deeply inspired by all their interesting things I learned and observed. ---------To see the genuineness of the people really touched me in their efforts to lend a helping hand. I am inspired when I go back to the U.S.A. to help more people and not expect anything in return. My purpose would just be to emulate the love of God." (Jeremy, CBU).

"This mission trip has impacted me personally on several levels. It has taught me to interact with people completely different than myself. It has also made me realize how fortunate I am and to never take anything for granted. Lastly, this mission trip has made me see the power of love and God working through everyone. The generosity and hospitality our group has received was amazing especially when we knew they didn't have a lot to give. I hope to come back next summer to continue the work we started and to meet with these people again." (Robinson, U of M).

There is no greater joy than to become a conduit of transformation in another human being's life especially that of a young adult. Any problems encountered in doing college ministry pale out in comparison to this joy. Following our second mission trip to Kenya in 2007 where we participated in the construction of one classroom to start a high school for Matharite village in central Kenya, I again invited students to make their remarks on their experiences. Here are excerpts from these remarks.

"I became so connected to the project that I felt like I was doing it for myself. It is amazing how the little work that I did meant so much to both the people of Matharite and myself." (Gideon, U of M)

"Most citizens of the US really don't know how blessed they are. I personally didn't know it until this life changing experience came about." (Marcus, EACC)

"This was truly a blessing and I look forward to next year! I have truly fallen in love with this country (Kenya), its people, and the people I have come with (fellow missioners). I have also fallen in love with God and his works all over again and look forward to continuing to grow in him" (Taralyn - CBU)

"To the individuals who made this trip possible, I would like to say Thank you, Thank you, Thank You, from the bottom of my heart. Because you gave so graciously you have impacted the hearts of hundreds, if not thousands. You have impacted the individuals who took part in the mission trip and the members of Matharite Village who will now have a high school to send their children to." (Willard - CBU)

It is most reassuring for any college minister, myself not exempted, to know that our ministry has motivated a student and moved him or her to own his/her faith in a new way. What else could a college minister ask other than to lead a student to fall in love with God? I couldn't ask for anything more than to know that in the course of my ministry as a college chaplain, I have motivated a student to pray and connect better with God and that through the process this student got better grades.

At the risk of resorting to a cliché, the world has become a global village. The more interaction we make with peoples from other cultures the more able we shall become to find our way in this global village. The more interaction we make with people different from us, the easier it will become for us to break the cultural barriers that have hitherto divided the world between "them" and "us." The more we make this interaction the more we come to realize that we are one people sharing one destiny.

Even more importantly for the young adults who are largely spoilt by the American materialism, international mission trips and interactions with other peoples give them a new perspective of happiness and materialism. Happiness is not contingent on materialism. In these mission trips, our students observed people who did not have a whole lot, but who carried a smile of gratitude for the little they have. Similarly, sharing is not contingent on the amount of material goods one has. It is a matter of spirit. The students again observed people who opened their homes and warmly welcomed guests, while readily and happily sharing their resources. There is no university that is capable of teaching these essential lessons of life. One has to observe and experience them.

These apparently simple lessons of life can be applied to the emerging global community to foster a spirit of togetherness and sharing. Most every conflict in our modern world has to do with the competition for resources. But it doesn't have to be that way. The world community can learn to share and be better stewards of the resources endowed to us by God. Modern warfare has shown how wasteful and destructive human beings can be. Again, it doesn't have to be that way. Human beings have great potential for building peaceful societies. Working together to build a health center or a school or an irrigation project is a good place to begin. As demonstrated from the feedback from our college students, mission trips build relationships and extended families. They stir love and understanding among peoples. They break stereotypes that divide peoples. They build trust and confidence needed to work together. It is most heartening to see this potential begin to unfold with our college students.

All it takes is the presence and faithfulness of the college chaplain in discharging his/her responsibilities as a servant of God. All it takes is for the chaplain to be there for students as they experience and go through their inevitable "takeoffs" and "crash landings" in college life as freshmen down to their graduation. It is reassuring for most students to know that someone really cares and journeys with them in their college life. That is what college ministry is about.

Chapter Seven

Leadership Recruitment Forum

"And how are they to believe in him of whom they have never heard? And how are they to hear without a preacher? And how can men preach unless they are sent?" (Rom. 10:14-15)

The gist of Paul's rhetorical questions is simple, if one wants to reach a goal; he/she must work towards that goal. If one wants to get to a destination, he must start moving towards that destination. In the absence of that, people can talk all day long but nothing will ever happen. It is like prayer, we can pray all day long, but we must also closely listen to God's voice answering the prayers we make. Sometimes God says to us rise and do ABC. If we are not listening, as we often don't, we continue staying put when our prayer has long been answered. We continue staying put when God clearly said, "take your pallet and walk."

In situations like those, we keep wondering why God has not answered our prayers while it is we who have either refused to listen to what God has said or failed to obey what he commanded us do. We get mad with God and blame him for our woes when the truth is that we are to blame for not listening and not doing what God commanded we do. In the same way, the Church can lament all the day long wondering why there is a shortage of young adults in Church. We can lament all the day long wondering why the youth are not responding to the call to the ordained ministry. The reality is that if we think that these things are important we must do something about it. We must facilitate forums for God to call young people. We must deliberately shift from being gatekeepers to ushers for our young adults.

Young Adults' Programs

Research shows that the Church in general and the Episcopal Church in particular, has a wide variety of ministries with young adults. The Episcopal Church, for instance, has a fully financed department in Higher Education, a ministry with Young Adults. This is a carry over from the Episcopal Society for Ministry in Higher Education (ESMHE). The latter was formed in the 60s as an advocacy organization for college chaplains and students in a time when college ministry was threatened with financial trimmings across the board. The society did an excellent job as the only organization where new college chaplains could turn for training, consultation and support. As a member of ESMHE and later board member, I am one of the beneficiaries of this organization before it was finally phased out, to transition to the new Higher Education Ministry with Young Adults.

Under the umbrella of the Ministry in Higher Education department, there are several organizations geared to reaching out to young adults. It is surprising that one hardly hears about these departments and their role in the Church. I suspect that the debate on human sexuality usurps most everything else, good or bad, that the Episcopal Church is doing. The debate on human sexuality gets all the coverage as if nothing else took place in the whole period of ten or so days of the General Convention. The leadership of the Church may have to devise a different method of communication or simply declare a moratorium on the debate on human sexuality for one or two General Conventions to put other agendas on the radar of the communicants of the Episcopal Church and society at large.

Pastoral Leadership Search Effort (PLSE)

One such Episcopal program is the Pastoral Leadership Search Effort (PLSE). The Office of Young Adults points out that discernment is something we do as a community. Through our relationships with others, we listen and tune in to what God might be saying to us. We do not discern on our own. PLSE seeks to identify young persons who might have the skills and interests to pursue an active role as lay or ordained leaders in the Episcopal Church. PLSE seeks to promote and provide conversations, occasions, and resources for vocational discernment and leadership development opportunities among the 16-30 year old constituency of the Episcopal Church. PLSE provides a different sort of community - one in which young people from all over the Episcopal Church join in conversations about discernment through blogging and community of mentors.

The office of Young Adults Ministry points out that there are 48 million people between the ages of 18 - late 30's in the U.S. with energy, ideas, creativity and passion. It must be the priority of the Church to empower this generation of young adults to use their gifts for the benefit of people and the purposes of God. The office believes there is a dynamic opportunity for young adult ministry in each Episcopal geographical region. It is the goal of the office of Young Adults to provide the resource necessary to unlock the potential in our young adults.

There is no doubt that PLSE is a noble program. The implementation of this program with young adults takes place in college ministries. College chaplains work with the office of Young Adults to reach this goal. The Church should be fully engaged in more of these types of ministries with young adults. Unfortunately, these kinds of efforts tend to be swallowed up by other more pronounced but equally divisive agendas of the Church.

Discernment Retreats

In Province IV, one of the ways this shift has started to take place is by having annual discernment retreats. These are forums where college students gather and with the help of others, discern whether God is calling them to the ordained ministry. This is a good start. One would hope that every Province in the national Church and every diocese would encourage a forum like this where young adults are encouraged to seriously consider the ordained ministry as a vocation. But my sense is that even this attempt is half-hearted. The Church must not only encourage but also facilitate and make it easier for young adults to hear God's call to ordained ministry. The Church must also actualize that call by making the discernment process less strenuous and seminary training affordable. Sometimes the discernment process is like an inquisition. What is desirable is an effective process that assures us of getting genuinely called persons to the ordained ministry. My role as college chaplain was to encourage my students to attend these discernment retreats. Where possible, I helped my students raise the necessary financing to attend these retreats.

Parish Discernment Programs

Some parishes such as St. Michael's Episcopal Church, Dallas, already mentioned above, have discernment programs that cater not just for their young adults but also for young adults across the nation. The parish provides scholarships to enable prospective students to go through this process. The process includes regular participation in worship services and community services. I have had the honor of recommending three college students through this process, two of whom ended up in going to seminary.

Community Living Programs

The Church has a variety of community living programs. The purpose of these programs is to expose students to a community service based on spiritual life. In addition to performing assigned community services, young adults also engage in a spiritual life of worship and study.

It is easy for many young adults to be self focused and believe that everything is about them. Community living programs help young adults to step outside themselves and see the reality of life. The experience challenges the young adults to ask themselves what they can do to make the world a better place. It is hoped that this process leads to vocational discernment for some of these young adults.

Seminary Open Houses

Seminaries also hold open houses where prospective seminarians visit seminaries and meet with faculty and students. The open house gives a first hand experience of a seminary setting. Prospective seminarians get to ask questions on programs of their particular interest. This is not unlike what happens in college recruitments. Students and their parents visit colleges of their own interest. They meet faculty, staff and students. They get a feel of the campus. They may even meet with the financial aid department staff and ask about the process of acquiring financial aid. These visits are crucial in determining a student's choice in seeking admission in a particular college. It is the same for prospective seminarians.

Discernment Committee

Normally, the stipulations of the Commission on Ministry (COM) are for parishes to set discernment committees for prospective candidates to the ordained ministry. Committee members journey with the candidate for a period of anywhere from three to six months. During that time, the committee asks questions to the prospective candidate and also encourages him/her to do the same. At the end of this period, the discernment committee writes a report to the COM or to the bishop giving their recommendation of the candidate.

This process normally works well in a parish setting. But for college students who are normally away in college or in a "foreign" parish may not feel comfortable with the process. That is why the General Convention gave consent for college communities to be allowed to serve as discernment communities. After all, for most college students, it is in college that they cultivate a meaningful spiritual relationship with their chaplain. It is here that some of their talents emerge and are employed in serving others. Putting up a discernment committee for such a prospective candidate makes good sense. Recommendation for such a person could either go to the local bishop or to the candidate's home bishop who no doubt has been kept abreast with the process from the beginning.

Internships

The Episcopal Church sponsors both domestic as well as international internships. Some of these internship programs are short while others may be as long as one year. The goal of these internships is to expose potential seminarians to Church ministry in real life. Students live and work with clergy and communities of faith who are engaged in the kind of vocation the student aspires to do. The program on the whole is affirming to such a young adult's call to the ordained ministry. The opposite may also be true. It may be that after going through the whole process of discernment and internship a young adult may find that church ministry is not where God is calling them. That is also all right. The ordained ministry is not for every person. The primary purpose is for the Church to provide opportunities and forums for young adults to hear and discern God's call to them.

Chapter Eight

Barth House is Closed

"You have looked for much, and lo, it came to little; and when you brought it home, I blew it away. Why? Says the Lord of hosts. Because of my house that lies in ruins, while you busy yourselves each with his own house" (Haggai 1:9)

In this and other remaining chapters of this book, I will mainly present the correspondences that culminated to the closure of Barth House and the reactions that followed. I will on the whole let the facts speak for themselves. I do not write this chapter in order to change any of the things that happened. Indeed I cannot do so. But I believe that the people who love and care for college ministry particularly in the Diocese of West Tennessee are entitled to these facts. I hope that those who read this account will judge for themselves the merits or lack of merits of the so called "evaluation process." What could otherwise have been a good scientific research turned out to have two primary objectives --- getting rid of the college chaplain and closing Barth House, and effectively terminating college ministry in the Diocese of

The Rev. Dr. Samson N. Gitau

West Tennessee. I begin with a recap of the Barth House facility and ministry.

Background

Barth House is strategically situated at the corner of the busy Patterson Street and Watauga Avenue. Directly across the street on the eastern side is Smith Hall, one of the women's dormitories at the U of M. Next to Smith Hall is Mynders Hall, another women's dormitory. On the northeastern side is the Panhellenic building, the busy Greek center for sororities and fraternities. Next to it is the new Fedex Fogelman Center. On the northern side is a student parking lot separating Barth House from the large Richardson Towers that houses most of the resident students at the U of M. The Towers also houses all the Resident Life staff offices. Directly across Watauga Avenue on the southern side is the Church of Christ college ministry house, recently acquired by the University of Memphis. On the western side is a residential house owned by the University. Most of the religious houses at the University of Memphis are lined up southwards along Patterson Street, starting with Barth House, Church of Christ, the Presbyterian Place, and the Baptist House. Behind the Baptist Center are the Rivers' Edge, the United Methodist House and the Roman Catholic House. One block behind the Wesley Center is the Hillel House, the center for the Jewish students. A Muslim mosque is two blocks behind Patterson on the western side. Of all these religious houses at the

Pitfalls

University of Memphis none of them is better situated than the Barth House in terms of student accessibility.

As already pointed out, Barth House has one of the best chapels at the University of Memphis. It's ideal for worship and small weddings. The sanctuary is furnished with a beautiful pipe organ and a baptismal font imported from England. The facility has a library cum dining room used for meals after services. It's also used for Bible study and other meetings. The room has an internet hooked computer and printer for student use, in addition to a big TV screen for student entertainment. The adjoining kitchen is always supplied with snacks, coffee, tea, and chocolate for students' use. The refrigerator always had a jug of ready-made pink lemonade and ice tea. The facility lacks room for student recreation such as ping pong and pool table, amenities available to some of the other religious houses at the University of Memphis.

When I was called to serve as the director of College ministry in the Diocese of West Tennessee, Barth House served as my office. The University of Memphis continued to be our central focus. I went out from there to do programs at Rhodes College, Christian Brothers University and LeMoyne-Owen College. I made an effort to build a diverse community by inviting students from these other colleges to come for Sunday worship and fellowship at Barth House. Students from other colleges such as Crichton College, Rust College, and South West Community College, also participated in these services. In the racially polarized city of Memphis, this was no small accomplishment to have students, white, black, rich and poor, Americans and non-Americans worshiping God and enjoying fellowship under one roof. I cannot think of a better way to foster racial healing than getting young adults to worship and work together. Throughout my nearly ten years of college ministry in the Diocese of West Tennessee, I deliberately made this one of my primary goals. It was therefore one of my saddest days to read from the *Daily Helmsman* that Barth House was closing down. It was hard to conceptualize all those opportunities and the hard work we had put into it thrown into the drain. But far from being a surprise, the *Daily Helmsman* article was the culmination of a long and methodical process. Here is a chronology of events.

On Thursday, February 1, 2007, *The Daily Helmsman*, the student run newspaper at the University of Memphis, carried the following article (quoted in full by permission):

The Barth House may be closing in June due to budget cuts made by the Episcopal Church, By: Kendall Jones, Staff Reporter (http://www.dailyhelmsman.com/news/2007/02/01/News/)

When she was a freshman, Rachel Robinson didn't have a car and could rarely leave campus.
Still, the junior double majoring in creative writing and Judaic studies found a way to make it to church.
"I didn't have anywhere to go but Barth House," she said.

Soon, she and others at The University of Memphis may not have that.

Pitfalls

The Episcopalian campus ministry has only been allocated half of their operating budget for 2007, according to the Episcopal Diocese of West Tennessee Web site.

For the building at 409 Patterson St., that means closing.

"Barth House will be shut down as of June," Robinson said, who is president of the Barth House. "If they're going to take that away, where else are students going to go?"

According to Stephanie Cheney, diocesan operations director for the West Tennessee office, students can continue to go the same place they always have.

"We're not planning on closing Barth House," she said. "We are considering a budget that does have some implications and budget cuts in certain areas. It's been given a different implication than what it really is."

Cheney said the Diocese is having "funding issues" that will affect, but not fully eliminate, the college ministry.

Two days a week, students can find home-cooked meals at the house, including worship services on Sunday and Thursday night Bible studies - all of which could be subject to change.

Rumors have also circulated through the campus Episcopalian community that the Rev. Dr. Samson Gitau would lose his job of nine years as chaplain.

"We want to have the best ministry that we can there," Cheney said. "There are no secrets here at all. As far as we are concerned, Samson is a part of that."

The budget, Gitau said, tells a different story.

Barth house used $136,885 to operate their full college ministry in 2006, according to the budget.

This year, their original proposed budget increased to $146,381 but was later cut down to $65,395.

Cuts in the budget include the clergy housing allowance ($33,000 to $16,000), stipend ($23,000 to $11,000) and campus ministry development ($12,000 to $0).

Gitau said the same thing happened in 2005, but the money was later restored when the house brought a group of college students to the conference.

The formal decision to cut the budget will come down from the Diocesan Convention in two weeks and, though Gitau is scheduled to meet with the Bishop of the West Diocese today, he is pessimistic the money will come again.

"Since 2003, our church has been going down in a lot of ways," he said. "We've been losing membership. I just seriously hope they can come up with the money."

As the chaplain, Gitau also holds Bible studies at other college campuses around the Memphis area.

Robinson said she thinks there is more to the story than simple budget issues, but she hopes, for the sake of students, the diocese will rethink their cuts to the budget.

"On average we reach about 100 students a week," she said. "As Episcopalians we can't compete with places like Bellevue. We have smaller numbers, but we have faithful people."

Rhodes College

The *Daily Helmsman* article led me to reflect on how the four multi-campus ministries I had started in 1998 had been gradually downsized to only two colleges. It started with Bishop Johnson declaring that in an attempt to give me the chance to concentrate on the students at the

Pitfalls

University of Memphis, he had decided to assign Rhodes College to St. Mary's Cathedral. The Reverend Katherine Bush, a newly ordained deacon, was assigned to render services to the students at Rhodes College. Bush was a suitable candidate for this job. She was herself a graduate of Rhodes College.

Without much thought and grateful that the Bishop had lessened my load, I relinquished my ministry at Rhodes College to Reverend Bush. Not that I had much choice in the matter. Not long after her appointment, Bush was ordained priest and called as associate to her home parish of Holy Communion. The Bishop then asked Ms. Clarisse Schroeder, a member of St. Mary's Cathedral and a lay chaplain at St. Mary's Girls School, to serve as part time chaplain at Rhodes College. She did. But a few months later, Clarisse was admitted to seminary. Rhodes College was left without any Episcopal presence. CB, the dean of St. Mary's, was not interested in reaching out to Rhodes College. The responsibility had been dropped on his laps and he was neither interested nor able to assume that role. Assuming that the Bishop had perhaps forgotten to appoint somebody else to do college ministry at Rhodes, I twice reminded him that Rhodes College students were not being served. At first, the Bishop appeared genuinely surprised, but by the second time, I got the message. The Bishop was not interested in appointing somebody else to do college ministry at Rhodes. The parish- based visiting priest model of doing college ministry had failed. This led me to recall that prior to my coming to the Diocese of Tennessee, Grace/St. Luke's Church had tried to reach out to Rhodes College without success. The visiting priest parish-based model of doing college ministry had miserably failed at Rhodes College. To date, Rhodes College, a liberal

The Rev. Dr. Samson N. Gitau

arts college, where ten percent of the student body is Episcopalian, has not had any college ministry for more than four years.

Bishop Johnson visits with Episcopal students at Rhodes College

Barth House community poses for photograph

LeMoyne-Owen College

One would think that Bishop Johnson had learned an important lesson from the failed experiment at Rhodes College. In one of our conversations in his office he told me that he had decided to ask Fr. Bill Kelly, vicar of Emmanuel Church in South Memphis, to reach out to LeMoyne-Owen College together with his parish. Surprised, but again knowing only too well that it was the Bishop's call, I facilitated a meeting between Dr. Wingate, then President at LeMoyne-Owen, Fr. Bill Kelly and a member of Emmanuel church, Bishop Johnson and Canon Rene. The lunch meeting at LeMoyne-Owen went well and I was persuaded that between Fr. Kelly and his parish and with the support of LeMoyne-Owen staff the students at LeMoyne-Owen would be catered for.

As fate would have it, Fr. Kelly was soon hospitalized, and went through an operation. He left Emmanuel Church. Emmanuel was no longer certain of its own ministry having only recently been reduced to a mission. The congregation hardly had any energy or resources to reach out to its members let alone to college students in a neighboring college. That was the last we heard about LeMoyne-Owen College student ministry. The parish-based ministry model of doing college ministry had failed yet again. To the best of my knowledge, the Bishop never bothered to appoint or ask any other parish to reach out to LeMoyne-Owen College. To date, more than four years later, LeMoyne-Owen, the only black college in the diocese of West Tennessee, has no Episcopal presence.

The Rev. Dr. Samson N. Gitau

Closure of Barth House

I couldn't help seeing the publication of the *Daily Helmsman* article on the closure of Barth House as the culmination of attempts by Bishop Johnson to phase out college ministry, purportedly, for financial reasons. In January 18, 2005, I met with Bishop Johnson in his office where he informed me that Barth House would be funded for only six months. I had just returned from a three month sabbatical leave in Kenya where I had been nominated for the office of Bishop for the Diocese of Mount Kenya Central. The news from the Bishop was sudden and shocking. I asked the Bishop if it would be in order for us at Barth House to raise the remaining balance for college ministry funding. After some uncomfortable hesitation, the Bishop said "I guess it's OK as long as you do not go to the same people we are asking to fund the diocesan budget." I left the bishop's office with a gloomy feeling, but also encouraged that there was still a ray of hope that we could still save college ministry. I talked the problem over with my friends who decided to support our efforts to save college ministry. By the time we went to the Diocesan Convention gathered at Grace/St. Luke's, March 4-5, 2005, we had raised enough money to fund college ministry for three more months. But we still had three more months to cover.

The Diocesan chairman of the board of finance presented the budget with a three month deficit for college ministry. The Diocesan Convention debated the budget and clearly indicated the importance of maintaining the full funding of college ministry in the diocese. By divine intervention, Holy Trinity, one of the local parishes, had a college student, Josh, as part of

Pitfalls

their delegation. Josh made a persuasive case on what Barth House meant to him personally and to other students in general. The delegates carefully listened and the Convention declined to pass the budget without the full funding for college ministry. Consequently, the Convention which was due to end before lunch was forced to adjourn for lunch and come back for more discussion on the budget. During the lunch break, Bishop Johnson conferred with the chairman of the board of finance, the diocesan chancellor and a few other advisers. The mood of the convention was clear. Delegates wanted college ministry fully funded.

When the Convention was called to order after lunch, lo and behold! the money had been found! The bishop had $120,000.00 from the sale of St. John's Church property in Martin, which surprisingly was designated for college ministry. If Bishop Johnson was indeed interested in funding college ministry it is a mystery of mysteries that he had stashed $120,000 in the bank from a sale of a diocesan property designated for college ministry and yet claimed to the Convention to have had no money to fund college ministry. It was not until he was placed in a tight corner that he divulged his well guarded secret. In retrospect, I cannot help but conclude that for whatever reason, Bishop Johnson had decided to phase out college ministry as early as beginning of 2005. Nothing was going to stop him from this goal. Money was only a convenient excuse to this goal.

About $20,000 of the newly found money was applied to bridge the budget balance for college ministry in 2005. The rest was distributed to run over a period of the next five years specifically for college ministry. I went home from the convention with a most grateful heart for the support I had received from the lovers of college ministry. But if I thought that the battle was over, I was wrong. More was yet to come. I had inadvertently embarrassed the bishop. Like an elephant, Bishop Johnson was not about to forget the experience. If anything, the embarrassing experience had only hardened his resolve to phase out college ministry in the diocese. He would however need to strategize more carefully than he had done.

College ministry did not become an issue in the 2006 budget. Money was easily found to fund it. But again, if I had thought that the Bishop's resolve to phase out college ministry and my position was over, I was wrong. The fight would surface again. This time the bishop's blow would be lethal. In my view, the bishop was only buying his time and carefully strategizing his next move.

College Ministry Study

In one of my meetings with Bishop Johnson in the spring of 2006, he informed me that he intended to institute a study for college ministry. It was going to be conducted by George Yandell, an associate at Calvary Episcopal Church, assisted by Alyce Craddock, who had prior working relationship with George. The study would be funded from a grant by the Church Home Trust. The Bishop suggested that I submit a few names of persons to be included in this team. Members were to visit various college ministries to establish what was

Pitfalls

high performing and what was low performing. I was not invited to this committee even though I was the director of college ministry and the only active college chaplain in the diocese. Barth House was also not one of the colleges to be visited for this study.

I welcomed the idea of the study. In my naiveté, I saw in this study an opportunity for us to show how well we were doing at Barth House in relation to other college ministries throughout the nation. I also trustingly told myself that the intentions behind this study were good and that they were intended to improve on what we were already doing. I talked with George Yandell and asked him to ensure that college students were represented in the proposed study. I pointed out that since it is the students who best know what their needs are and how they are being met, any report on college ministry should involve them. George did not honor my request. Of the names I suggested to George, only one, Ms. Lavonnie Perry-Claybon, was included in the team to conduct the study. I recall asking George whether the team would visit Barth House. George told me that they wouldn't visit Barth House. The process started in June 2006. I was never at any time informed how it was progressing, the campus ministries they had visited, the data they gathered or how they sought to interpret it.

The first draft of this study was ready in December 2006. The Bishop invited Fr. Yandell alone to present this preliminary report to him and Canon Somovidella. I was not invited to this presentation even though I was the main stake holder in its outcome. Even more surprising, the Bishop invited selected members of Yandell's group to present the report to Bishop and Council at St.

Columba, just before they approved the final budget for 2007. For the record, Lavonnie Perry-Claybon, the Barth House liaison, was not invited to this presentation.

I was also not invited to the meeting of Bishop and Council where the report on college ministry report was going to be presented. This was curious due to the fact that an issue that had a direct bearing on me and my ministry was going to be discussed without me having seen the report or given a say in it at all. In my view, the omission was not accidental. The presentation was one sided and it was meant to be that way. Looking back, there is now no doubt in my mind that the purpose of this presentation with only a selected number of Yandell's team invited to participate was to influence the decision of Bishop and Council in its budgetary decision. From the Bishop's email to me referenced below, it's evident where the bishop stood on this matter. He already hailed the report as "very good" and "fascinating." Yet, up to that point neither I nor members of the College Ministry Board had seen it. From a reliable source, George Yandell's team plotted a "bell curve" which they used to show that Barth House was below the curve. It worked. Bishop and Council members were influenced by the report and went along with the Bishop to drastically cut the college ministry budget by funding it for only six months, January to June, 2007. The message was loud and clear after June 30, college ministry in the diocese would cease. It is mystifying that the learned members of Bishop and Council did not question George and his selected team members if they had ever visited Barth House or what criteria they had used to arrive to their conclusions. It is equally mystifying that these members did not question the original purpose of the report. Was it to improve on what we already had or was it to justify the phasing out of college ministry in the diocese? These are respectable and well learned members of Bishop and Council but I cannot understand why they failed to ask these crucial questions to the decision before them. I reiterate that up to that point neither I nor any member of the College Ministry Board had been invited to the two presentations. Our college ministry liaison and member of the team was not invited to any of the two presentations either. Was this a fair and open process? Was Bishop Johnson desperately seeking justification for something about which he had long made up his mind? College ministry in the Diocese of West Tennessee and my position as director of college ministry had to go. Again, it begs the question why and how the members of Bishop and Council could not have sensibly asked whether Barth House had been visited and how its ministry compared with those of the other college ministries visited. Furthermore, I had been made to understand that the purpose of the study was to improve on what we had already and not to kill it. There was no doubt that this was a case of self-fulfilled prophecy. In my view, the Bishop had already made up his mind. The termination of college ministry was *fait accompli*. The primary purpose of Yandell's report was merely a public relations smoke screen to justify the unjustifiable. It seems to me that Bishop Johnson had perhaps forgotten that justice must not only be done, but more importantly, be seen to be done. If one looked for justice and fairness in this whole process there was none.

The Rev. Dr. Samson N. Gitau

The day before Bishop and Council met I received an email from Bishop Johnson, dated Wednesday January 10, 2007. Here are the relevant excerpts

Dear Samson,

"I understand that you have recently requested copies of blueprints of Barth House. I imagine that this relates to some of the discussions we had a couple of years ago regarding the placement of student housing on site. It brings to mind that we will need to speak soon anyway regarding the outcome of the financial considerations for Barth House for 2007 (yet to be determined but soon to be proposed by Finance Committee) and of the struggles I am having with going forward with the Mission Trip for the coming summer (again a factor of what I anticipate is going to be hard to justify given the fact that we started our budget setting process for program for the diocese some $200,000 short of what we need.) We are having to make hard choices regarding the budget proposed to convention, and the money for a mission trip to Kenya is becoming less winsome as I ponder it. Also, I have some very specific ideas to discuss with you about the site of Barth House. We need the ministry, but do we need it on the current site?

We also need to discuss with George Yandell (and others?) the outcome of the very good study his group did regarding effective campus ministries around the country. I found the findings, even in their rough draft form, fascinating. I wonder what the implications will be for campus ministries across the state. I should have a better idea of what the financial picture for the diocese, diocesan staff and ministries will be by Thursday. I know

Pitfalls

that we are busily looking for ways to balance expenses and income. Given the current gap in funding, a number of options will inevitably be on the table."

In retrospect, this email is most telling as to where the Bishop Johnson was headed with college ministry. The writing was clearly on the wall. College ministry was on the chopping board. As soon as Bishop and Council was over on Thursday, Bishop Johnson called me to inform me about their decision to cut college ministry. He informed me that college ministry had been funded for only six months in the 2007 budget. I expressed my surprise to him given that Yandell's team had never visited Barth House. I insisted that the report was never an evaluation of college ministry at Barth House and in the Diocese of West Tennessee. Furthermore, I argued, it would be premature to conduct a research and spend $20,000.00 of Church money and not be able to implement the report to get to where we want to go. No amount of logic could persuade Bishop Johnson to change his mind, at least not yet and even then only temporarily. The die had been cast. The diocese was in a financial crunch, or so it was argued, and college ministry had to be chopped off. In retrospect, I now see that I was in denial. The Bishop's email from the previous day was clear on what I had to expect. I still trusted that my bishop was impartial! I was wrong.

The Bishop gave me an appointment to see him in his office for him to give me an official report on Bishop and Council's cut on college ministry budget. I met the Bishop in his office on January 18, 2007. He formerly informed me that he had seen the report and it was not good for college ministry. At that point the Bishop gave me a copy of the draft report that had been presented to Bishop and Council. Obviously, the report was meaningless to me now that it had been used to essentially terminate college ministry. In my conversation with the Bishop I once again asked him how a report that never targeted Barth House in its study, either by way of interviews or physical visit could be detrimental to what we were doing at Barth House. Bishop Johnson couldn't give me a convincing answer. For whatever reason, he couldn't see the glaring blunder he had committed. He had applied an untested report as pretext to cut college ministry in the diocese in order to balance his budget. After that meeting with the Bishop, I confirmed my worst fears that I was a man under siege.

I went home and shared the information with Lilian. I told her that I neither had the strength nor the courage to fight the Bishop's decision even though I knew it was clearly wrong. Soon my friends and supporters of college ministry heard about the decision to cut college ministry. They called the Bishop and protested the decision. By this time, rumors had started to spread that Fr. Samson's college ministry was only to Africans and especially to Kenyans. Those with open minds wanted to see first hand for themselves what all this was about. Mrs. Gillian Steinhauer came and worshiped with us. The following Sunday her husband, Dr. Steinhauer came with her. They stayed for dinner and interacted with the students after the service. They clearly saw the diversity we had created and enjoyed at Barth House. Even without telling me, they decided to do something about our financial problem. They gave a very generous donation of $15,000 towards

Pitfalls

the 2007 college ministry budget. Parish supporters of college ministry especially St. Andrew's and St. Philip's increased their donations.

The rumors regarding my ministry require mention. Even if it were true that most of our Barth House students were Africans, which they were not, one wonders why that would be conceived as bad for the Episcopal Church in West Tennessee. In a church that is 95% white, one wonders how it would be harmful to have one congregation in the diocese ministering to persons of color. Were the rumor mongers trying to have their cake and eat it at the same time? The Diocese cannot talk about diversity and justice for all and then complain that one out of thirty or so parishes was reaching out to persons of color. I find this deplorable.

I reflected on what the Bishop had said and then wrote him the following letter dated January 28. My purpose was to put things into perspective and to reiterate what I had already reported to the Bishop on what we were achieving in college ministry.

January 28, 2007

Dear Bishop Johnson,

Thank you for talking with me in your office on January 18 after the Bishop and Council meeting. It was hard for me to hear that college ministry will not be funded beyond June 30, 2007, in the proposed budget to be presented to the Diocesan Convention. I have dedicated myself to this ministry for the last nearly nine years. I would like to see it continue.

Bishop, in talking with you last week, you gave me to understand that the budgetary cut was mainly due to

The Rev. Dr. Samson N. Gitau

lack of funds. But now I hear that it is also a performance issue. Bishop, I am remiss of failure to comprehensively communicate to interested parties on what we are doing in college ministry. But I am a doer and not a public relations person. Maybe I should know better.

Bishop, we continue to operate full programs at both the University of Memphis and CBU. At the University of Memphis we have Morning Prayer, Monday through Friday, Holy Eucharist and lunch on Wednesdays, Bible study on Thursdays, choir on Sundays and Holy Eucharist, dinner and fellowship on Sundays. At CBU we have Bible study on Mondays, and Wednesdays and Noon Prayer on Thursdays. We are into community services, mission trips, conferences, teaching, baptisms, weddings, and counseling, to name a few.

Here is what this week (January 21-26) looks like in terms of programs and numbers.

1:00 P.M. Sunday worship	48
6:00 P.M. Holy Eucharist worship	15
Monday Bible study CBU	7
Morning Prayer Monday – Thursday	12
Wednesday Holy Eucharist	6
Wednesday Bible study CBU	6
Thursday lunch meeting CBU	7
Thursday Bible study, Barth House	4
Sub-total	115
Mailing list	240
Total	355

Pitfalls

These numbers neither include students who met with me individually in my office or transacted ministry via the email or phone. Nor does it include my presence at campuses, the students I talked to in the parking lot, or other meetings like the mission trip planning committee on Saturday.

Bishop, I have now seen Father Yandell's report and look forward to hearing more about it on February 6. It is a step in the right direction and an opportunity for improving college ministry in the Diocese of West Tennessee. Let's take it to the next logical step and apply it to what we are already doing. But even a casual look at this report affirms that in terms of numbers and programming, Barth House is high performing. Can we do better? Sure we can. Please give us the chance to continue building on the foundation we have already laid.

As you already know, I have written a two year grant request to start college ministry in the Jackson, Tennessee area colleges. The probability of this grant getting funded is high. I would be glad to see this dream come true and be a facilitator in this new beginning.

Finally, allow me to make five suggestions on how this opportunity may begin to look like.

a) Use Fr. Yandell's report to evaluate our current college ministry
b) Use the model to establish the proposed college ministry in Jackson, Tennessee.
c) Allow us to fund raise 10 -15 per cent of our college ministry budget starting with this year.

d) Advocate for us with the Church Home Trust to fund us for the remaining balance and thus complete the work they have already begun.
e) Give our students a chance to make a presentation at Convention, possibly after Fr. Yandell's presentation, and let the delegates hear first hand what college ministry means to our students.

I look forward to discussing these suggestions and others that you may have for me with you on Thursday, February 1. Thank you for your support in this ministry.

Yours faithfully,
Samson N. Gitau

These were touchable suggestions I was making to the Bishop with the hope that he was willing to help us demonstrate to the Diocesan Convention and other stake holders how much we had progressed in college ministry in relation to the colleges studied by George Yandell and his group. In retrospect, I now see that I was still very naive to think that my letter would make the bishop see things differently or even change his mind. I was naïve not to realize that the bishop had commissioned the college study to serve his own purposes. He had effectively used it to achieve his desired purposes long before I or the members of the College Ministry Board had been given a chance to see it. On the basis of this report, college ministry funding for the 2007 budget had been cut to only six months. After six months it was over.

Pitfalls

It was on the basis of this report and proposed budget cut that the article in *The Daily Helmsman* was written.

My reaction to the college ministry report was with much disbelief. The way it had been manipulated to achieve a certain end was shameless, to say the least. I convened a meeting of the College Ministry Board for us to go through the report and establish the meaningful differences. I was not about to give anybody an excuse to harm college ministry. I enlisted the help of one of the board members to conduct a survey particularly on the issues the report had addressed. The monkey survey required feeding it with emails of students who were to receive this survey. I decided that this was not enough. We made copies of the questionnaire and went to the student eating and hanging out places and asked students to fill out the survey for us. I talked to the administration on some of the issues raised in the report. These included: enrollment, demographics, retention rate and disciplinary problems. I talked to my colleagues in Religious Life Staff on some of the common issues such as "the ethos" of the University of Memphis and what the report called, *raison d'etre* "the reason or justification for existence." I shared our findings with the College Ministry Board. The board concluded that we were on the right track. Furthermore, most of the issues raised in the report are not the kind that one puts in place overnight. They are ongoing. So rather than ignore the report, we took it seriously and went ahead to implement it the best we could to gauge what we were already doing. In that regard, the report was helpful. But our efforts were inconsequential to the powers that be. Looking back, I now clearly see that nothing was going to change Bishop Johnson from what he had long decided to do –phase out college ministry.

The publication of *The Daily Helmsman* article led to all kinds of reactions from students and supporters of college ministry. These reactions are presented in chapter ten below. Some people called the Bishop on the phone and others wrote to him. Some came to our services to see first hand what was going on. Pressure was mounting on Bishop Johnson to keep college ministry afloat in the Diocese. Yandell's team was invited to make their presentation to members of the Church Home Trust and to the members of the College Ministry Board who had as yet to see it. The meeting took place at the Diocesan office. The Church Home Trust gave another generous donation. Enough money was found to fund college ministry for another six months.

By some coincidence, the day I had to go to see the Bishop in his office on February 1, 2007, *The Daily Helmsman* carried the article on the closure of Barth House. The Bishop's secretary saw it first and called the bishop to alert him about it. The Bishop and Canon Rene Somovidella, canon to the ordinary, were coming from some meeting in East Memphis. The Bishop immediately called me and asked if we could meet in my office that morning rather than for me to go down to his office in downtown. I agreed to this change of venue. In retrospect, it was godsend that we met in my office that morning. I have never seen Bishop Johnson as furious as he was that morning. He ranted that the *Daily Helmsman* publication was just the kind of thing that was not helpful to the diocese and to college ministry. I explained to him that I had nothing to do with the

Pitfalls

publication of the article. I pointed out to him that the students were concerned with what they were hearing and naturally wanted to know what was going on. In his fury, Bishop Johnson must have forgotten that America enjoys unfettered freedom of expression. The meeting ended with the bishop still fuming furious. The next time I was to meet Bishop Johnson was February 6, in the already scheduled meeting at the Diocesan office where George Yandell and his group were to make their presentation to College Ministry Board and other interested parties. It was most ironic that a group that had never visited Barth House and whose report had been effectively used to justify the cutting of college ministry budget and essentially the termination of my position, was making a presentation on the effective performance of college ministry to us.

Report Presented

The meeting was held at the Church House on February 6. Supporters of college ministry from Barth House and St. Philip's were in attendance. As it turned out, there were only two persons from Yandell's team, that is, George himself and Alyce Craddock. It begs the question why the others were not there. Was it a deliberate selection? Any way, the two arranged to have George Yandell make presentation to the members of the Church Home Trust and Alyce Craddock to the college ministry community. I was obviously in Craddock's presentation. The mood was tense. Ms. Craddock was hard-pressed to answer questions from the Barth House supporters present. They wanted to know the methodology used in the study. They wanted to know how it applied to our ministry at Barth House. Instead of answering the questions asked, Alyce insisted on reading the list of meaningful differences word for word in total oblivion that she was addressing literate people. Participants were not interested in the details of the report but in how it had been compiled and its relevance to Barth House and college ministry in the Diocese of West Tennessee in view of the fact that the team had never visited Barth House. Alyce could not answer these questions.

Meanwhile, upstairs in the Bishop's office, George was concurrently making a separate presentation to the Church Home Trust Board who had funded the research. Finally a case was made that given the additional funding from individuals and given the fact that it was necessary to gauge the effectiveness of our College Ministry at Barth House in the light of the report, it was only fair that the Church Home Trust make another grant to enable this process to take place. I argued that such a chance would allow us to demonstrate what was really going on in college ministry. Following this meeting, I wrote my suggestions to Bishop Johnson on how I felt the findings of the report should be applied. I left the meeting cautiously hopeful that somehow our case had been heard and that a permanent solution would soon be found. The following morning I wrote the following email to Bishop Johnson expressing my optimistic spirit.

Wednesday, February 07, 2007
To: Don Johnson
Subject: Thank you

Dear Bishop Johnson:

Thank you so much for your efforts in addressing our college ministry funding problem. I see this as an opportunity for us to improve on what we're already doing. I think the meeting last night was informative. The report has its shortcomings, but like I said last night, it is a step in the right direction and we are ready to use the tools it provides to evaluate where we are in the bell curve of those meaningful differences.

I very much appreciate the overwhelming support we are getting from all kinds of people in this ministry. I also appreciate those people who care enough like Dr. Bruce and his wife, Gillian, who have come to see first hand what is going on at Barth House. On Sunday 73 participated in our two services. For four and half years, I attended Sunday evening worship services at Boston University as a graduate student. In 1990/91 I was the interim Episcopal chaplain at BU. At that time Boston University had 800 Episcopalians. The largest number I saw in any one service in the course of those years was 22. We are witnessing 3-4 times as many in our Sunday services here at Barth House.

Can we do better? Certainly we can. I look forward to working with the College Ministry Board in exploring ways and means of improving on what we are already doing. I met with Fr. Bob van Doren yesterday and gave him the names of the college ministry fund raising task force. Thank you for asking him to chair this task force. I have no doubt they will do well. Thanks again for your support in this ministry.

Samson Gitau

Fund Raising

Two other good things happened from all this mess. At least it appeared to me at the time. Pressure from the supporters of college ministry led the bishop to appoint a six person Task Force charged with raising funds for college ministry for 2008. Members of this task force included: Bob van Doren, chair, Dr. Bruce Steinhauer, Paula Wood, Stephen Shelton, John Hannum and Bill Johnson. These are respected members of the diocese. Even more importantly, they all love college ministry. Each of these persons has had prior contribution to Barth House ministry in one way or another. For instance, as already pointed out, Dr. Bruce Steinhauer and his wife Gillian had made a generous donation to bridge the college ministry budget for the current year of 2007. It was this generous donation that persuaded the Church Home Trust to make a similar contribution in order to test the "meaningful differences" report with what we were already doing at Barth House. The College Ministry Board also undertook to work with the task force to complement their efforts to ensure a more lasting financial solution for college ministry in the Diocese of West Tennessee. So it appeared that with sufficient funds now available to cover the whole of the 2007 college ministry budget, the Task Force and College Ministry

Pitfalls

Board working in concert to trouble shoot for future college ministry budgeting, we were headed to a more lasting solution to our financial problem in college ministry.

The Diocesan Convention

Miraculously, funding for college ministry for 2007 had been found in full. The budget was presented at the February Diocesan Convention gathered at St. John's Episcopal Church. But even as the budget was presented, it became crystal clear that college ministry was still funded at the six month level. On raising this anomaly in the budget hearings, the diocesan treasurer explained that the Bishop had instructed him to have the budget presented that way. The fact was that funding had been found to run college ministry from January to December. But here were tea leaves with a message to read and decipher. In my optimism, I convinced myself that all was well. My son, Gideon, who was the vice-president of the Barth House student group and college student representative for Province IV, had more foresight in reading the tea leaves. He put it more succinctly, "from July to December 2007, Barth House will be operating on charities." Gideon's insight was profound. His insight was greater than mine. The message was clear, college ministry may have acquired sufficient funding for the year, but the Bishop's determination to phase out this ministry had not abated one bit. College ministry had been summarily eliminated effective end of June. The rest was a question of formalities. Bishop Johnson would soon see to these formalities. Unknown to me and the Barth House community, the formalities to close Barth House would not wait the end of the year. They would come sooner than any of us could have anticipated.

The Bishop gave the college ministry study committee a chance to make its presentation to the Diocesan Convention. The committee took a whole two hours to make their presentation. Although I had hastily prepared a report entitled "Barth House Highlights' outlining what we were specifically doing at Barth House and the number of students we were reaching, I was not given the chance to make my report, even though I requested the Bishop in writing for the opportunity to do so. The best I was allowed was to give copies of my report to the Diocesan staff to pass on to the convention delegates. At the end of Yandell's presentation and before the end of the Convention, the Bishop distributed evaluation papers for delegates to fill specifically on the college ministry study report presented. The evaluations still remain under lock and key in the Bishop's office. For the sake of transparency, one would hope that Bishop Johnson would share the result of these evaluations with the college ministry stake holders including myself and the College Ministry Board. It would be interesting to see what the delegates had said about the presentation. It seems to me that the sole purpose of the report was to impress the convention on the low performance of college ministry in the Diocese of West Tennessee. In my view, the main purpose for this presentation was to tie the trimming of college ministry budget to performance.

In his address to the Convention on the college ministry problem, the Bishop praised the work of the study committee and the good work they had done. He said that the work was an unprecedented and that it was going to be a great gift to the whole Episcopal Church. I still wait to see this happen.

The Task Force

No doubt reacting to the many letters, emails and calls made to him by communicants in the Diocese, Bishop Johnson announced to the Diocesan Convention the formation of a task force of six persons to specifically work on the college ministry funding for 2008. The appointment of this task force was a great relieve to me. I had no doubt that these persons had the ability and will to raise the necessary funds for college ministry. These are reputable persons in the diocese and truly care for college ministry. My hopes were soon to be shattered.

At the time, the Bishop appeared to have some confidence in the role he had assigned to the task force. In an email to me here is what he said about this task force.

Tuesday, February 13, 2007
To: Samson Njuguna Gitau
Subject: Thank you

Samson,

I just got back in town today, and am catching up on emails. Glad Church Home was willing to help us out along with the others you mentioned for a short-term solution to funding short-falls.

The Rev. Dr. Samson N. Gitau

I hope Bob Van Doren's group will focus more on the ongoing funding needs of campus ministry beyond 2007.

Blessings and I look forward to seeing you at convention.

Don

Again, my assuming trust was getting the best of me. I convinced myself that the Bishop meant what he said. I was soon to find out otherwise. Perhaps as naive as me, but no doubt in very good faith and love for college ministry, once they had been officially appointed by the Bishop at the Convention, the eminent members of the task force took their task seriously. They held two meetings, June 6 and July 18. Here are minutes from the two task force meetings.

Minutes of College Ministries Fund Raising Task Force June 6, 2007

Attendance:
John Hannum, Bill Johnson, Steve Shelton, Paula Wood, Bob Van Doren.
Absent: Bruce Steinhauer

The first organizational meeting of this Task Force met at 4:00 p.m. at Saint John's Episcopal Church.

Certain questions were asked about the historical nature of the funding of college ministries in the diocese

Pitfalls

and none of us were totally aware. It was agreed that Chairman Van Doren would contact Kim Teel in the diocesan office to receive answers to these questions.

The committee explored certain methodologies available for fund raising which would include a possible Capital Funds drive which could be incorporated into a larger Diocesan-wide funds drive where the funds allocated for college ministries would be endowed and the income used to partially fund the annual operations.

There was discussion about individual parish giving and the need for a 'College Ministries Sunday' during the year to increase congregational awareness of this program. Comments were made about setting up a Barth House Outreach committee focusing on the work of Barth House students involved in the community and thus receiving funds through grants from humanitarian trusts in the city of Memphis. Also an annual golf tournament was also discussed as a way of raising money. The Emmanuel Center Golf Tournament raises about $30,000 a year.

Most of the members present will be able to attend the Fund raising for Campus Ministry seminar put on by Anne Ditzler of the Episcopal Church Foundation in New York to be held on Saturday, June 30, from 9:00 to 1:00 at Barth House.

The committee will meet again to discuss further the particulars relative to where we will go to search out funding opportunities.

Respectfully submitted
Bob Van Doren, Chairman

The Rev. Dr. Samson N. Gitau

Minutes College Ministries Fund Raising Task Force July 18, 2007

Attendance: Bill Johnson, Paula Wood, Bob Van Doren.

Absent: John Hannum, Steve Shelton, Bruce Steinhauer

Because of the small turnout of this meeting, no specific actions or recommendations were made.

Discussion centered on a recap of Anne Ditzler's presentation on June 30 as well as the chairman's visit with the Bishop on July 12. Of course, the budgeting process for 2008 has not yet begun so the amount of diocesan funding for College Ministries is still under review.

With an annual budget for Barth House at $100,000, a case could be made to keep the Diocesan funding at the same level as 2007 ($67,000) with the remaining amount ($33,000) for to be raised from individual contributions and parishes.

However, it could be argued that funds set aside for college ministries should address development of ministries on other college campuses in the Diocese beside the University of Memphis. If the latter scenario is preferred, then alternative sources of funds will need to be explored: such as a parish led outreach ministry with nearby campuses where the parish would share the expense of the college ministry with the diocese.

Those in attendance at this meeting agreed that it would be impossible for this task force to take on any larger commitment than $33,000 for 2008 as time is running out for appealing to an existing donor pool made up of 75 individual donors and two parishes from the diocese.

Pitfalls

Given proper direction from the Diocese and a better understanding of the program offered by this ministry, a definitive plan for funding can begin to develop that will be in place for the 2009 funding year.

These initiatives would include approaching corporations and non-profit foundations for contributions and motivating students on campus to engage in community outreach programs and through these efforts to raise grants from other community non-profit organizations.

The Task Force plans to meet again in mid-August after other interested parties have met to give this committee further feedback and input

Respectfully submitted,

Bob Van Doren, Chairman

There is no doubt from these minutes that the Task Force was determined to find a solution to college ministry funding for 2008 and beyond. The Task Force had no shortage of ideas to reach this goal. Regrettably, this was not to be. Bishop Johnson summarily killed this committee soon after its second meeting. One can only wonder why Bishop Johnson could not allow members of the Task Force to finish the work he had assigned them to do.

Fund Raising With Ditzler

In an attempt to trouble shoot college ministry funding, I asked the College Ministry Board to have us work with

The Rev. Dr. Samson N. Gitau

Anne Ditzler of the Episcopal Church Foundation in New York. Our efforts would complement those of the Task Force and others seeking solution to college ministry funding. Anne has worked with many college chaplains helping them to fund raise for their ministries. I had talked with her and she had agreed to work with us. The board consented to this proposal. They agreed to meet Anne's expenses for the training. I approached the bishop and informed him what we had planned to do and to get his blessings. The Bishop gave us the green light to proceed with this project.

The training was scheduled for June 30, 2007. Anne asked me to furnish her with documentation of our ministry which I did. She finally came and conducted the college ministry training. Twelve persons were in attendance including members of the task force. It was evident that our double pronged approach to the college ministry funding for 2008 and 2009 was on track to success. However, for whatever reasons, Bishop Johnson was not willing to give these efforts a chance. As pointed out above, no sooner had the task held its two sittings that summer than the Bishop called Bob van Doren and told him that he had disbanded the task force with immediate effect. The Bishop had arbitrarily disbanded the task force he had himself formed before the Diocesan Convention. I was not personally given the courtesy of being informed that the Bishop had killed the task force let alone why he had done it. Even more discourteous, neither Bob nor the Bishop formerly informed the members of the task force that their committee had been disbanded.

Pitfalls

The Bishop also prematurely killed Anne Ditzler's work with us. Anne had written a report to the Bishop indicating that if the fund raising efforts were to succeed, the diocese must be involved. Her report affirmed the findings of the Task Force that the diocese must assume a percentage of the college ministry budget and only have the College Ministry Board and other efforts such as the task force raise the rest. It was evident to me that Bishop Johnson was not ready to continue funding any portion of the college ministry budget. It again, begs the question why Bishop Johnson was unwilling to give these efforts a chance if indeed he wished to continue college ministry in the diocese. Why did Bishop Johnson kill a committee he had himself created? Why did he abruptly terminate the fund raising project with Anne Ditzler, that he had given a green light? Did the Bishop fear that these combined efforts were going to succeed where he did not in reality want them to succeed? Did he fear that the success of these efforts would thwart his real intentions to terminate college ministry in the diocese? Bishop Johnson did not bother to explain his actions.

Chapter Nine

Evaluation of Barth House

And the Lord said to me, "Amos, what do you see?" And I said, "A plumb line." Then the Lord said, "Behold I am setting a plumb line in the midst of my people Israel; I will never again pass by them" (Amos 7:8)

In the first week of August 2007, Bishop Johnson invited rectors of the big parishes and persons of interest in college ministry. I was exempted from this closed door meeting and only came to know about it after it had taken place. The topic of discussion was titled "Thoughts on various campus ministry models." The clergy invited to this meeting included: Don Brooks, Sean Ferrell, John Moloney (late rector of Grace St. Luke's), John Sewell, Rene Somodevilla, Bob van Doren and George Yandell. Also invited but could not attended were Fr. Andy MacBeth and Mark Rutenbar. Following this meeting, the bishop wrote a summary of the meeting to these participants, giving me a copy of the summary. Attached with my copy was a cover letter addressed to me. The cover letter said in part:

The Rev. Dr. Samson N. Gitau

"In the course of the meeting, it also was clear that the group wanted to know when the Barth House ministry evaluation would be carried out. This was particularly based on the hope that the funding issues for various campus ministry offerings across the Diocese would best be addressed sooner, rather than later, in preparation for 2008 funding. I agree, and the evaluation plans in broad-brush terms are spelled out in the attachment. I wanted you be aware of the dates and plans as well."

I applaud the group meeting with the Bishop for bringing to his awareness that up to that point, no evaluation of the Barth House ministry had been conducted in light of George Yandell's report or for any other purposes for that matter. The only evaluation conducted was by the College Ministry Board, but whose results were obviously not recognized by the Bishop. Bishop Johnson had finally acknowledged what in his undue haste to use George Yandell's report as pretext to terminate college ministry as early as December 2006, he had ignored to have an evaluation conducted on this ministry. He had at last acknowledged that no evaluation had been conducted on the Barth House ministry either by using the flawed study or any other criteria for that matter. Bishop Johnson continued to acknowledge this fact in his summary report to his college ministry group. The report says in part:

"In 2006, we were blessed to receive a generous grant from the Church Home in the amount of $20,000 to make an assessment of effective campus ministries in a number of locations, looking at styles and approaches currently in place. The assessment was also to include a recommendation for implementation of the findings as a means of enhancing and making more effective our current and future campus ministry programs. This study and its recommendations have taught me a lot. George Yandell, as he noted in his comments to you, has identified a set of "meaningful differences" that make for thriving campus ministries. These findings look different in different locations, but there is a check and balance effect that allows for flexibility in programming in order to effectively address student-based needs in any particular setting. Our Church Home funded assessment, and the recommendations coming out of it, are the basis on which the effectiveness of our current and future campus ministry will be evaluated."

The evaluation of the University of Memphis ministry's implementation of the "meaningful differences" will be done in mid-September (George, Sean and others will be part of this process.") God willing, it will be completed and recommendations will be made by early October for the future direction of the U of M (Barth House) ministry so that leadership and budgeting implications for the Diocese can be addressed in the 2008 proposed diocesan-wide campus ministry effort."

The Bishop's letter concluded: "It is hoped that the September evaluation will demonstrate that "the meaningful differences" have been put in place in time for the opening of school and that its current incarnation will be sustainable in the future. I look forward to hearing the results.

Thanks again for your thoughts and input.

Blessings,

Don."

The Rev. Dr. Samson N. Gitau

At last Bishop Johnson had acknowledged what I had all along insisted. No evaluation of college ministry in the diocese had been conducted thus far. The next logical thing to do was for Bishop Johnson to graciously apologize to Bishop and Council for knowingly misleading them as early as December 2006 to believe that Yandell's report had been applied at Barth House and effectively shown that we were below the high performing level of college ministries. He should have graciously acknowledged that using the report to cut college ministry in 2007 was a mistake that should have been immediately corrected. Instead, the bishop set a time line to, in my view, justify an injustice that had long been done with dire consequences for college ministry in the Diocese of West Tennessee and to my position as director of college ministry.

For now, suffice it to say that Bishop Johnson had given an evaluation timeline of about two months. The Bishop's letter to me of August 8, 2007, continues to elaborate on the college ministry evaluation process.

"I wanted you to be aware of these dates and plans as well. However, I would encourage you to call George Yandell and schedule a meeting between you, George, a member of your board, and others George has invited to be involved in the evaluation, as funded by the Church Home. The members of the Church Home are interested as well in the results of your efforts to put in place the "meaningful differences" that they funded."

Again in my naiveté, I trusted Bishop Johnson to do the right thing and to honor the process he had laid out. However, I found it disingenuous that Bishop Johnson was asking George Yandell, the same person who had authored the fictitious report and who had made no less than four presentations to the Bishop, Bishop and Council, The Diocesan Convention and the Bishop's August 2007 group, to come and conduct the evaluation. In all those presentations George had not hidden his bias against what we were doing at Barth House. The bias had caused irreparable damage to college ministry and to my position. Did Bishop Johnson truly expect that George would seriously change the course he had taken? It is like somebody who has been unfairly indicted, condemned and sentenced to make a passionate appeal for a hearing only to be given the same impartial judge to hear his case again. What had changed? I could not help but conclude that George was Bishop Johnson's hireling to implement the Bishop's plan. He was an agent to do the Bishop's dirty job. There was no doubt in my mind that George could never be a neutral evaluator of college ministry. He had repeatedly demonstrated his lack of impartiality. I wrote to the Bishop and pointed out George's lack of impartiality and asked the Bishop in an act of fairness to appoint someone else to conduct the evaluation. My letter to Bishop Johnson dated August 13, 2007, was in reply to his letter on College ministry evaluation.

August 13, 2007

Dear Bishop Johnson,
Thank you for your letter dated August 8 calling for an evaluation of our current ministry. I warmly welcome this opportunity. As you rightly point out, this week I

The Rev. Dr. Samson N. Gitau

enter my tenth year of college ministry in this Diocese. I love this ministry and continue to do it with dedication. I look forward for the opportunity to share with others what we have done and what we are currently doing and what we plan for the future. I am heartened to know that some clergy colleagues are conversing with you on how best to continue improving and supporting college ministry in the Diocese.

In the interest of fairness, I ask that Fr. George Yandell withdraw himself from the evaluation process and that, you appoint a more neutral person to chair this process. I have no problem with you appointing any of the other clergy that met with you, namely The Rev. Mssrs. Sean Ferrell, Bob van Doren, Don Brooks, John Sewell or any other member of the current College Ministry Board to chair this evaluation process.

One of my comments and request after receiving Fr. Yandell's report was that the committee had done its work and should now hand over the results to the College Ministry Board for implementation. This remains my request. The committee had the opportunity to present the report to you personally, to Bishop and Council and to the Diocesan Convention. It's now time for the College Ministry Board to interpret, assess and implement the report in light of what we are doing. Indeed, the College Ministry Board has already begun this process.

Furthermore, an evaluation of college ministry should not be confined to one report. The committee should be free to formulate its criteria of evaluation that allows it to reach an informed and independent conclusion.

With these two requests, the timing is right and I look forward to putting a small group together to work with the chair and team from the Diocese in bringing this process to a successful completion.

Thank you for your continued support in this ministry.

Yours faithfully,

Samson N. Gitau

Bishop Johnson neither acknowledged this letter nor my requests to him. My plea for fairness went unheeded by my own bishop whom I would have expected to protect my interests. If Bishop Johnson had any interest whosoever on being fair-minded, one would be hard-pressed to see any trace of fairness here. The next thing I heard was a call from George Yandell on August 31 giving me dates for the evaluation committee meeting. The meeting was urgently scheduled for Thursday September 6. I sent an email to three members of the College Ministry Board asking them to participate in this meeting. Here is my email dated August 31, 2007.

Dear Bindy, John and Lavonnie,

Bishop Johnson has asked me to put together a subcommittee to work with another he has appointed to evaluate College Ministry. This process will take place in the months of September and October. The first meeting has been scheduled for Thursday September 6, 2:00 P.M

The Rev. Dr. Samson N. Gitau

at Barth House. I am writing to kindly ask you to serve in this sub-committee. I realize that this may not be the best time for some of you, but also want you to know that your presence and support for college ministry is always most appreciated.

Blessing on each one of you.

Samson Gitau

I also invited Rachel Robinson, the Episcopal Student Organization president at Barth House and also the student representative in the College Ministry Board. Come the meeting date, the diocesan team arrived at Barth House. They were Fr. Sean Ferrell, rector of St. Luke's Episcopal Church, Jackson, Tennessee, a former college ministry chaplain, prior to his coming to the Diocese of West Tennessee, Fr. Joe Alford, also a former college ministry chaplain, and Alyce Craddock, the "professional" co-author of the "meaningful differences" report with George Yandell.

I was relieved to find that Bishop Johnson had sent Sean to chair the meeting. In my optimistic spirit I anticipated fairness in the evaluation process. But it soon became clear that Sean had neither an agenda nor a sense of direction on what the committee was supposed to do. Time was spent seeking clarification on the criteria to be used on the evaluation process. None was given. I explained to the committee how seriously we, that is, I, and the College Ministry Board, had taken the report and the steps we had taken to address the questions raised in Yandell's report. Some of these steps included a monkey survey of the U of M students. I shared the questionnaire and the results with the committee. I pointed out how we had already begun implementing the other concerns in the report. I shared our weekly programs and the numbers of student participants. Using these numbers we were able to demonstrate how far in Yandell's bell curve we were. We were certainly not in the low performing area even from the controversial bell curve Yandell had plotted. The meeting was over in one and half hours with no mention of what was next for the committee. I felt comfortable that we had demonstrated how we had implemented and were continuing to implement the report with all is flaws.

My relief was short lived. On September 14, 2007, I received a call from Bishop Johnson with an urgent and stunning message. The evaluation report of college ministry was out and it was negative. I couldn't believe what I was hearing. The Bishop explained that he had received the report from the evaluation committee and it was devastating to college ministry at Barth House. I said to the bishop that may be he was talking of a different meeting other than the one I and the members of the College Ministry Board had participated in. I told him that in that meeting we had clearly demonstrated how far in Yandell's bell curve we were in terms of student numbers and the steps we had taken in implementing other concerns in the report in the two weeks of the fall semester that had just begun. The Bishop invited me to his office for the official report from the evaluation committee.

Looking at the report, I can only say that it was not worth the paper it was written on. It was sham. I cannot believe that up to now neither Sean Ferrell nor Joe Alford has come forward to dissociate themselves from this sham of a report. For starters, the one page cover letter was signed by none other than, you guessed it, George Yandell, who was neither in the meeting nor ever been to Barth House to either interview me, my assistant, as Bishop Johnson had suggested, or even more importantly, the students at Barth House. How in the world could somebody who was never in a meeting sign a report and present it as factual?

Second, neither Rev. Bindy Snyder, nor Ms. Lavonnie Perry Claybon, nor Ms. Rachel Robinson, the three members of the College Ministry Board participating in the meeting were either there or consulted when the report was written. That leaves only three people to have written it, that is, Sean Ferrell, Alyce Craddock and Joe Alford. Whereas, I have no doubt that Alyce was George's crony, it remains a mystery what role Sean Ferrell and Joe Alford played in writing this report. If there was a single person who should have written the report, it ought to have been Sean as the chair of the meeting. If he had written it, fairness dictates that he should have shared it with all the others members of the committee and have them sign it before presenting it to the Bishop. This never happened. Participating members of the committee neither saw the report nor even knew that they were to write one. It therefore begs the question as to how a report supposedly by a committee of six persons excluding myself could have been usurped by three persons and at worst one person. The report writers had neither shame nor scruples. One wonders what was in it for them to sacrifice their integrity to write such a sham of a report. How could they have done this while knowing so well that the fake report would lead to a man losing his job and to students losing their program? Again, Sean and Joe have yet to say what role they played in writing this report. How could these clergy persons knowingly crucify one of their own? Assuming that they did not write this report, as I would wish to persuade myself to believe, why do they still remain silent knowing well the consequences of their false report? Silence means consent. Are both Sean and Joe silent accomplices to a scam hatched by George Yandell, a hireling of Bishop Johnson or did they truly believe in what they wrote? Were they shamelessly willing to indict, sentence and crucify an innocent person?

Finally, one recalls that the time-line for the evaluation was September and October. Did Bishop Johnson forget his own time-line? How could a two month process have been accomplished in one sitting? Even more importantly, how can one evaluate a college ministry without ever interviewing the student participants in that college ministry? Is this what George and his team had done in the colleges they had visited? The report was a shameless demonstration of self-fulfilled prophecy. It was clear indication how low these people were willing to stoop in order to terminate college ministry and my position as director of college ministry. For this to happen in a church that blasts its own trumpet on human rights is the cruelest perversion of justice I have yet to see.

The Evaluation Report.

The cover letter of the evaluation report dated September 13, 2007, seven days after the meeting was as follows:

The Rev. Dr. Samson N. Gitau

Dear Bishop Johnson,

On September 6, Sean Ferrell, Joe Alford and Alyce Craddock met at Barth House with Samson Gitau, Lavonnie Perry Claybon, Bindy Snyder and Rachel, a student leader. This is the formal report to you and for the others with whom you wish to share.

During this two-hour "Go and See for Yourself" meeting (see Pages 31-32 of the report "150 Days-Engaging Students in Episcopal Campus Ministries' of August 2007) the trio above asked, generally and specifically, about Barth House's progress in implementing the meaningful differences.

What we learned falls into three buckets:

1. What Progress Has Barth House Made Towards Systematically Putting Each Meaningful Difference in Place? (Recommended step to Question Themselves Aloud. Progress: *Not Evident/Only Anecdotal, In Beginning/Early Stages, Midway, Fully in Place*)
2. What Hide-Behinds Did We Hear Barth House Leaders "Hiding Behind"?
3. What Obstacles Mentioned By Barth House Could Be Removed?

Yours respectively,

George Yandell, facilitator, Campus Ministry Development Team

Pitfalls

The 13 page evaluation report had a sliding scale of four:

1. Not Evident, or only anecdotal 2. Beginning, Very Early stage 3. Midway 4. Fully.

It also had a column for progress Notes.

Of all the items addressed in the report they were all marked in scale one, that is, Not evident or only anecdotal. The only two exemptions were:

1. *Characterizing prevailing stress gestalt for students attending University of Memphis* and 2. *Characterizing the prevailing ethos at the University of Memphis.*

Everything else, including "Providing inclusive hospitality" for which Barth House is well known for was anecdotal! Our clear mission statement which ironically still headlines the college ministry page in the diocesan website was also given an F grade. Simply put, the evaluation committee had shamelessly handed me an F on my score card. I have been a student for many years, but never before from elementary to graduate school did I ever get an F grade. I have not ceased to wonder whether it's me who received the F grade or whether George and his team of "professionals" did not inadvertently give themselves an F grade.

I recently read a story of some guys who went out hunting. One of them spied a moose. The guys shot through the bush until all sounds ceased. Upon investigation, these guys discovered only the body of a man. Then they remembered hearing during the commotion of their moose shooting a voice saying "Don't shoot. I'm not a moose." In retrospect, they realized that the "moose" had been waving a red cap.

The Rev. Dr. Samson N. Gitau

It dawned on them on what they had done. They had killed a helpless man.

The tragic story illustrates how sometimes people become so fixated in their ideas and goals that they become totally oblivious even to blaring contradictory information. Some people tend to see what they want to see. They tend to hear what they want to hear. Even more tragic, long after the evidence has clearly demonstrated the truth, some people still cling to their wrong ideas and actions. George's cronies had come to Barth House to "Go and See for Yourself." They no doubt saw what they wanted to see or perhaps what they had been instructed to go and see. What is worse, they still refuse to wipe their eyes to see the reality of the human casualty they have caused.

One would only hope that after seeing the lifeless body of nearly ten years of a college chaplain's career brought to the grave, and after seeing a thriving ministry with students who must now live without any Episcopal presence, and after seeing the selfish sale of a students' property that has been serving students for over eighty years sold, the moose hunting guys will finally be remorseful.

I recall writing an email to my friends telling them that I had been given an F grade. One of them was gracious enough to see humor and different meanings in the F handed to me. It meant: Freedom, Faith, Fellowship, Family, Financial blessings. I don't know about some of these meanings, but I certainly know that it did not mean what it was intended to be. As adjunct professor of religion at the U of M, I grade students. I take time to explain to my students what I am looking for in a

Pitfalls

particular question. At the beginning of the semester I clearly explain in the syllabus my grading criteria. I also take time to review with the students before the quiz. What I saw with George and his cronies was a sham like no other. He writes in part: "What we learned falls into three buckets." This implies that the writer, George, was present in this learning experience. He signs the letter to that effect knowing fully well that he was not there. I leave it to the reader to judge Yandell's actions. But I find it most embarrassing that Bishop Johnson takes pride in the likes of George and their mediocre performance.

The evaluation report had the desired effect. The effect was fast and methodical. In his telephone call to me on Friday September 14, Bishop Johnson summoned me to his office on Monday September 17 for the official report card. He had invited Canon Rene, canon to the ordinary for this meeting. It soon became evident that at this point the question was not how the committee had arrived at the devastating report. It was not whether the right procedure had been followed. It was not whether the Bishop's time-line had been exhausted. It was not even whether Barth House students were ever consulted. Apparently, the Bishop was satisfied with the correctness of both the method and the results used to write the report. Apparently, the Bishop had forgotten that he had given about two months to mid October for the evaluation process. All that was history now. The question was not even how we could implement any of the areas presumed to be deficient in the report. Again, the Bishop had apparently forgotten the purpose of the college ministry study of meaningful differences which was in his own words "to better our performance in doing college ministry in and beyond the University of Memphis." The Bishop effectively gave me a red card. I had been dismissed from the game. The Bishop generously gave me exactly 13 days to wrap up college ministry. The doors of Barth House would thereafter close down. In the words of Bishop Johnson, he was doing me a favor. Failure to close Barth House sooner than later would leave him having no money to pay for my terminal sabbatical leave. The Bishop had slammed the red doors of Barth House closed.

Chapter Ten

Reactions to Closure of Barth House

"Panic and pitfall have come upon us, devastation and destruction; my eyes flow with rivers of tears because of the destruction of the daughter of my people" (Lam. 3:47-48)

After my meeting with Bishop Johnson in his office on September 17, things started moving very fast. It was my responsibility to inform the college ministry community, about what the Bishop had decided and what to expect. In an email I sent to the Barth House community dated September 18, 2007, here is what I said:

Tuesday, 18 September 2007
From: Samson Gitau
To: Barth House Community

Dear friends:

Greetings. After the initial shock, I am now in a better position to let you know that after meeting with Bishop Johnson yesterday, a decision has been reached to close

The Rev. Dr. Samson N. Gitau

Barth House effective October 1. I find it very ironic that the doors of Barth House close when Barth House is making a very effective impact on the campuses at U of M and CBU.

Last week alone, we held a 9/11 memorial service at the University Plaza where over 200 students/faculty and staff attended. 31 persons participated in Bible study and 80 persons participated in our three worship services at Barth House. The numbers for the previous week are similar.

A report chaired by Fr. Sean Ferrell on September 6 gave us an F grade in our performance. It is unbelievable that even our signature ministry of hospitality is given an F grade. The Bishop said that "I am running Barth House like a mission." So it is not that we are not reaching out to the students. It is not even that we do not have enough programs between 3 bible studies, two full worship services, not to mention Morning Prayer, Monday through Thursday, but that we are not doing it to the liking of some people.

As I look back these nearly 10 years of college ministry in this diocese, I do so with lots of gratitude. Looking around I have realized that I am one of the oldest serving clergy in the diocese. Others have come and gone, or found me around. Lilian and I are most grateful for this great opportunity. Our joint resolution from the beginning of this year has been to always see our glass as half full and not as half empty. So I see this as an opportunity to move on to what else God has for me. I hold no grudge against any person even those who have deliberately and knowingly twisted and misrepresented facts to suit their purposes. I forgive them from the bottom of my heart.

I take this chance to thank you all so so much for your support, moral, time, financial, and friendship which you have freely given us in this ministry. My heart goes out for the students who have found in Barth House a home away from home, and a place where they can be nurtured.

Please pray for them and may God bless you abundantly.

In Christ,

Samson Gitau

As I reflected on the closure of Barth House and effectual termination of college ministry in the Diocese of West Tennessee, I recalled the story of Joseph in the Hebrew Bible. Joseph had been sold by his brothers as a slave in Egypt. In slavery, Joseph established himself and earned favor with the Pharaoh. Eventually the Pharaoh welcomed the whole of Joseph's family, his parents and even the bothers who had sold him in Egypt. Under this Pharaoh, Jacob's family thrived and multiplied. But as the story unfolds, the writer points out that the Pharaoh died and was succeeded by another Pharaoh who did not know Joseph. The new Pharaoh did not recognize Joseph's contribution to the Egyptians. Instead, he was afraid of the Hebrews. His fears were that these people would continue to multiply and eventually be joined with other Egyptian enemies to wage war against the Egyptians. So the Pharaoh and his advisers devised a way to decimate the ever increasing Hebrews. That in a way is my story.

I came into the Diocese of West Tennessee in August 1998 invited by the college ministry search committee to come and do college ministry under the leadership of Bishop James Coleman. College ministry was the brain-child of Bishop Coleman who had solicited funds that funded my position. The funds were given by an anonymous family from Grace/St. Luke's. They gave it as seed money to plant the work of college ministry in the Diocese. The diocese in return provided the facility and the balance of the funds for my position. Bishop Coleman was most supportive of college ministry. One of my apprehensions however, was the realization that Bishop Coleman would retire in our fourth year of college ministry in the diocese. After that I wasn't sure what would happen.

Eventually, a search committee was appointed to look for Bishop Coleman's successor. The final five nominees came for a walk through of the diocese and an opportunity to meet with clergy and laity of the diocese. The walk through was held on Friday, March 16, at Holy Communion. Interested parties asked the candidates questions related to their particular ministries. I recall asking Fr. Don Johnson what his vision for college ministry was. His answer was that I was the one doing college ministry and he would do his best to support me in what I was already doing. I felt assured and went ahead and voted for Don to succeed James Coleman as Bishop for the Diocese of West Tennessee. Don was a compromise candidate. The more orthodox delegates were inclined to vote for Fr. Martyn Minns from Virginia. The liberals were inclined to vote for Fr. Zabron A. Davis, III, of Mississippi. When it became evident that neither camp was going to have their candidate, a compromise candidate was elected. I personally felt happy with the election and with my vote. We had elected a former college chaplain, or so he had introduced himself. He had assured me that he would support college ministry. As I was to soon find out, Don Johnson will promise something today and act as if he never heard about the promise tomorrow. I can cite multiple instances, including his now infamous vote against the election of Gene Robinson as Bishop of New Hampshire in the 2003 General Convention. A few days later in a diocesan debriefing of the General Convention gathered at Grace/St. Luke's, Don reversed himself and profusely apologized to the gay community in the diocese for letting them down with his vote. It is as if Don had never known the existence of the gay community in the diocese before voting against Gene Robinson. A meeting with the rectors of the major parishes in the Diocese a few minutes prior to the debriefing had led Don to see the light. He has never been the same.

In a second email I wrote to the Barth House community dated September 21 here is what I said:

Dear friends,

Greetings and best wishes to you all. This has been a hard week in many ways. It started with a meeting with Bishop Johnson on Monday morning where he told me his decision to close Barth House effective October 1. That gave us 13 days' notice to wind down. The students, faculty, staff and friends of Barth House and myself, of course, have not taken it easily. We have dedicated ourselves to this ministry for nearly ten years now and to close it down is hard. I have received emails, phone calls, and visits from all kinds of people - college chaplains, fellow clergy, students, parents, friends of Barth House, faculty and staff, all expressing their disappointment in the decision to close Barth House. The first to call me early on Tuesday morning was Dr. William Porter, Dean of students at the U of M, who well knows my contribution in college ministry. The other to call me was Brother Rob, the director of college ministry at CBU, and a great supporter of our Episcopal ministry there.

Others have written to the Bishop asking him to reconsider his decision and the impact it is likely to have on the students we serve. But as I told Bishop Johnson, I have no intention at all of becoming a stumbling block for the vision and plans he has for the diocese. What I clearly know is that God closes one door only to open another. History and the Bible are full of examples of this. So I know that God has wonderful plans both for the students we serve at the U of M and CBU and for me personally. In spite of the distractions, our programs have continued well this week. We had 78 attend worship, 26 in Bible study, not to mention the personal contacts we have made in the eateries and other gathering places. I need to emphasize that these numbers are not the same persons recycled. They are different persons in each of the programs, except me, of course. Of the new students we had in our programs this week, one is from Germany, another from India, another from Korea, another from Cameron, and yet another, the son of one of our diocesan workers.

Pitfalls

Like I have said before, Barth House is the most diverse congregation in this Diocese of West Tennessee. Our membership comes from: Germany, Australian, China, India, Korea, Romania, Latin America, Africa (a wide variety of African countries), and of course Americans, both Black and White. When I came into this diocese in 1998 one of my goals was to build a diverse campus ministry. I have achieved this goal and this is the legacy I would like to leave behind. I hope that the Bishop and the Diocesan Leadership will find it in their hearts to continue this legacy with or without me.

Thank you so much to all of you who have supported and continue to support and attend the programs we have at Barth House and CBU. This could not have been possible without your faithful support.

Finally, we still have two Sundays to worship together. Come join us on Sunday as we thank God for the ministry he has given us these nearly ten years. Join us as we pray for God's guidance in the days ahead. Our service begins at 6:00 P.M followed by dinner and fellowship.

Peace to you all.

Samson Gitau

Friends and Supporters of College Ministry

Lavonnie Perry-Claybon was the only member of Barth House community invited to participate in the college ministry study. As already pointed out, Lavonnie was also a member of the College Ministry Board and student adviser. She is one of the three members of the

College Ministry Board who were there at the so called "evaluation committee" on September 6. Here is what Lavonnie had to say about the evaluation report (quoted by permission).

Monday, September 17, 2007
To: Samson Njuguna Gitau, et al.
Subject: RE: F Grade

Hello everyone,

This is a praying time. I was a part of the ministry team that went across the U.S. visiting other college ministry programs. After reviewing the reports from others and seeing the ministry that I attended, I was proud to share what a wonderful ministry that we have for our college students in the Memphis area. As I reflect on that meeting, I am even more disturbed by the meeting and the misrepresentation of data and comments in the report to the Bishop. As a Christian, I am concerned, and I have lost some deep respect for the individuals who represent the Lord and were a part of the misrepresentation. The manner in which the meeting was run was very disturbing. The questions were not presented in a manner that would be pleasing to God; At least, that is my feeling.

The deed is done! Where do we go from here? It would have been great to see the Bishop work to develop a transitional plan for meeting the needs of the students. Students have enough stress and the closing of the Barth House with only a two week's notice adds to that stress.

I am planning to organize a prayer vigil for the students. If you wish to participate in that vigil, let me know. This is indeed a praying time. Also, if you have any other ideas, please feel free to call me at (I have omitted the telephone number).

In His service,

Lavonnie

The Reverend Bindy Snyder, another of the three members of the College Ministry Board present at the so called "evaluation committee" reacted as follows:

Monday, September 17, 2007
To: Samson Njuguna Gitau
Subject: Re: F Grade

Dear Samson,

That is very strange news and truly came as a surprise to me. I will be happy to write in your behalf, or whatever you think would be of help. I'm so sorry you are going through this. You do work hard.

Bindy

Rachel Robinson's reaction to the report is presented below in her letter to the Bishop. She, too, strongly disagreed with the report presented to Bishop Johnson by George Yandell. She describes the report as biased and fictitious. It is remarkable that all three members of the College Ministry Board disagreed with the report and yet Bishop Johnson praised it as good evaluation. No amount of pleading with Bishop Johnson could make him give the report a second thought. Instead he wrote to the diocesan communicants declaring that college ministry had been evaluated and found wanting. I leave it to the reader to decide whether or not this was the reaction of an impartial person? In my view, the Bishop was determined to get what he wanted no matter what it would take.

The *Daily Helmsman* of September 18, 2007 carried yet another article titled: "Barth House Closing" by Amelia Sewell, Staff reporter (quoted in full by permission).

The Barth House Episcopal Center, built in 1967 and located on Patterson, is to close in two weeks. Barth House officials said it is closing because of financial concerns.

Samson Gitau has been the Barth House's chaplain for 10 years and said he is deeply upset by the closure of the house.

"The Barth House has been able to offer student's worship, Bible study, retreat and mission," he said.

Under Gitau's tenure, several members have been married at the house and he has taken multiple group mission trips to Kenya.

The house offers morning Prayer, weekly Bible study and Sunday services. In 1995, University of Memphis student R. Foster attended the Barth House, because he was looking for morning prayer.

Despite graduating from the U of M in 1996, Foster remained active in the house.

"I usually help with anything they might have helping the students, like freshmen move-in week," he said. "I

Pitfalls

home school my daughter, and I also bring her to the services."

Lavonnie Perry-Claybon, student adviser, has been actively involved with the Barth House for about seven years. "I am just really sad it is closing because this has been a ministry to the students," she said, "I'm just disappointed at the process and lack of communication."

Claybon feels Bishop Don Johnson needs to make a plan for the transition period instead of just closing the Barth House's doors to its members.

"Students are already under enough stress as it is and to come to church and it just be closed to you, does not help," she said. As Christians, we need to care for each other. The bishop needs to put together a team with the old and new members that can meet the needs of the students."

Gideon Njuguna, the vice president for the Barth House, is equally upset with the news. "I have been to all the other student houses and haven't found one that compares to Barth House," he said.

Still, for some the news is not a complete shock. In February, an announcement came that the Barth House would be closing in June, but later the decision was reversed after a story in *The Daily Helmsman*.

I've seen it coming because the current bishop has not been very supportive of the Barth House," Njuguna said. "It's just because of dirty politics that it's closing, but it is not going to break up what we have at the house."

The Rev. Dr. Samson N. Gitau

Njuguna said he is planning on continuing to meet with students who are willing, once the Barth House closes. Claybon said she does not think financial reasons are enough excuse. "Budget is important, but we should work together," she said. "I know we need to be financially able to support ourselves but I am disappointed we are not working to keep this open.
Bishop Johnson could not be reached for comment.

Other reactions were made directly to Bishop Johnson in writing or via emails. Some of these people were kind to give us copies of their emails or letters to Bishop Johnson. Others called him on the phone, the content of which may never be known to us. Here is a cross-section of those reactions.

Wednesday, September 19, 2007
To: Bishop Johnson
Subject: Barth House

Bishop Johnson...

I am shocked and saddened to learn that Barth House will be closing effective October 1. Having moved back to Memphis from Purdue University where Nina and I were very active in the Episcopal campus ministry there, we saw first hand what a blessing this small ministry was to the students at Purdue.

Having left the Memphis area for Purdue and knowing the wonderful work that Father Samson Gitau provided the Memphis students, we sought out the Purdue campus ministry! And that congregation of young students and scattering of "older" folks made for a blessing for both Nina and myself!

Please do whatever you can to keep this ministry going. The Episcopal Diocese of West Tennessee cannot do with yet another closing of an important program...or afford to loose the ministry of Father Samson... We must continue to be there for the young. They are indeed our future...

The priorities of the Diocese must be for keeping the Barth House open and thriving...not closing.

Len

Wednesday, September 19, 2007
To: Ran Foster; et al
Subject: Thank you so much

Dear Friends, I am getting ready for a fund-raiser for Samaritan Counseling Centers this weekend - but we need to contact the Bishop's office to see whaT WE CAN DO TO KEEP BARTH HOUSE OPEN. iF THE CHURCH DESERTS OUR COLLEGE CAMPUSES WE'RE IN MORE TROUBLE THAN I'VE THOUGHT. MAYBE IT CAN BE KEPT OPEN LONG ENOUGH FOR US TO CONFER WITH THE BISHOP AND DO A BARTH HOUSE MERGENCY FUND-RAISER OF SOME SORT.

jO

Thursday, 20 September 2007
To: Bishop Johnson
Subject: Barth House

Dear Bishop Johnson,

I am in the midst of Samaritan Center's fund-raising at the moment, but what can we do to keep Barth House open and Father Gitau's ministry ongoing? I can't imagine that the diocese would suddenly cease having a presence in the institutions of higher learning here in Memphis. And Barth House has had a long and vital role among our next generation.

With concern,

Jo

Thursday, September 20, 2007
To: Samson Njuguna Gitau

Dear Friends,

I am forwarding you a letter that I have sent to the Bishop asking him to please reconsider closing Barth House. Please pray for this ministry and Samson and his family. Please consider sending the Bishop a letter with your input on Barth House. I feel certain that he didn't make this lightly, but it is such an important time in the lives of these kids, and to take away this loving and caring option for a safe place to meet and find Christ, is incredibly sad to me.

Blessings,

Susan

Thursday, 20 Sep 2007
To: Bishop Johnson
CC: Rene, et al
Subject: Barth House

Dear Bishop Johnson,

I have just received the very shocking and sad news that the decision was made to close Barth House. While

I feel certain that you did not make this decision lightly, I would like to appeal to you to please reconsider this and leave Barth House open.

Our world today is full of rigidity and religions that have become bean counters for God's good side and tickets to heaven. One offering that our wonderful Episcopal church gives, especially to questioning students, is a place to experience God's loving presence and develop a relationship with our Lord without all of the judgment. I dare say that no other student ministry at U of M allows this, and Samson Gitau has been a very faithful servant of Christ and that campus of seekers.

What would we need to do as a body to keep this ministry and Barth House open? I just cannot believe that this decision is right, and so I am compelled to write and ask you to please reconsider, and help us know how to help you keep Barth House open. I think there is an army of people out here who feel strongly, and we would be willing to pitch in, so please give us some options.

As always, you are in my prayers and I hope that you receive this letter with the loving intentions with which it is sent.

Your friend in Christ,

Susan

Thursday, September 20, 2007
To: Donald, et al.
Subject: Letter to the Bishop

Susan's letter inspired me to email a letter to the Bishop as well. Mine is a more personal letter that I'm only sharing with people who know me well, so I would appreciate your not forwarding it any further.

I truly hope that we as a Christian community can avoid Barth House's closing. I think Johnny's idea is a good one - that as many people as possible who support Samson and Barth House attend Sunday evening service there on September 23.

Melissa

In due respect to Melissa's request, I have declined to quote the more personal information of her letter to Bishop Johnson. But she too made a strong and compelling case against closing Barth House. Melissa concludes:

"Would you (Bishop) please let us know what we can do to bring Barth House back? I have served on Cursillo teams with Samson, and I have seen how dedicated he is to his ministry. I believe Barth House and Samson's ministry are needed now more than when he first started here 10 years ago. He provides understanding and guidance for people who are students, transients and those who are traditionally underserved by established churches, by offering education and worship and missionary opportunities.

I urge you to reconsider your decision to close Barth House. Its loss will create a void that would be difficult or impossible to fill in our diocese."

Wednesday, September 19, 2007

Pitfalls

To: Peter, et al
Cc: Samson Njuguna Gitau
Subject: Thank you so much

Dear Liturgical Friends

Barth House may be a mission as defined by Bishop Johnson. We are dealing on the fringe with folks that are liturgically mobile. We must recruit these folks unless we are to become extinct frozen-chosen. It greaves me to see St Elizabeth on stage Road Closed and St Paul's on Watkins tettering on the edge, St Anns (Milington) not serving the mixed neighborhood. Those are not elite neighborhoods and too many blacks. They are not our kind. WE are not providing for the religious needs of the under class and the blacks. They are finding church homes in their own in liberal thinking black churches and even Bellevue Baptist now has about 10% Afro American i am told by the grape vine by an Afro American. Memphis is an Afro American city and if we are to stay here we need to cultivate the group that Barbara Bush called un-class. The chosen -frozen-white Church will surely die in Memphis in the next 15 to 25 years.

Sam

Calvary

Wednesday, September 19, 2007
To: Samson Njuguna Gitau
Subject: Hello

Fr. Gitau I am so sorry this happened to you and the students who you brought to the Lord. I am not surprised, Bishop Johnson has gone on a different path than many of us expected. John and I left the Episcopal church about a year ago and we have never looked back. We now attend Faith Anglican church and dearly love it.

You have been a blessing to many and I believe God will find the perfect spot for you. I remember when we attended Cursillo and you were one of the spiritual directors, you heard my confession and I was so impressed with you.

God's speed Fr. Gitau, keep in touch and let us know where you will be.

Sharon

From Clergy Friends

Some clergy colleagues also called or wrote to Bishop Johnson appealing to him to reconsider his decision to close Barth House. Of course others would rather not write a letter that would appear to challenge the bishop's decision even though it may be wrong. Others wrote directly to me. Here are a few letters from those who were courageous to do so.

Tuesday, September 18, 2007
To: Samson Njuguna Gitau
Subject: Thank you so much

Dear Samson,

It is with a heavy heart that I learn of your news. I don't see how he can do this. I will ponder and search for biblical parallels. I hurt for you, my friend, that you should be treated dishonorably, when you have been the most

Pitfalls

honorable of us all. God loves you, and he knows you, and he will put you to good use somehow. May he bless you and your dear family now and always.

I pray for Gideon, that he not be made too bitter for your sake. Thank you for giving me the trip in which I became his friend and in which I became your brother. Maybe we will do it again sometime.

What does the future hold? Do you have a plan for the next few months?

Faithfully,

Joseph+

Wednesday, September 19, 2007
To: Samson Njuguna Gitau
Subject: Barth House

Dear Samson,

I was so shocked and sorry to hear that Barth House will be closing in a very short time. I can't imagine the Episcopal Church not having a presence on the campus after all these years. I took my first EFM training there in 1989 and of course have attended numerous meetings there. You have been such a faithful priest to the students, faculty and others who have come to Barth House for a variety of reasons. I am sorry not only about the closing but also about how you were evaluated and then informed of the decision. I work for a large hospital corporation which also often handles personnel matters in what I think of as a "cold" way, as they are always looking to the budget and ways to cut to make the budget. One would hope that the Church would be more pastoral, but it has not been my experience that this is so. My own unpleasant time happened at the Cathedral in November, 1997, and it opened my eyes to how the Church can be viewed as just another business by many of its communicants and also by some of the clergy. Fortunately, a group of folks at St. Mary's rallied around Dean Cooper and myself and prevented us from being let go at the end of the year or else having salaries vastly reduced.

Please know that you and Lillian are in my prayers, and I hope something positive can come out of this for you. You are a valuable asset to our diocese.

In Christ,

Nancy.

Wednesday, September 19, 2007
To: Samson Njuguna Gitau
Subject: Are You Being Tested?

Samson+

After we hung up the phone with you we all (Ruth and John Urban, Mary and Bp. John Githiga, and Bp Gideon Githiga) prayed extensively for you. We thanked God for many "F's" for you: Freedom, Faith, Fellowship, Family, Financial Blessings, etc. These are the real blessings for you. Those from Bishop Johnson are false.

I'm forwarding my devotion of the day to you.

We appreciate you and honor you as a brother in Christ.

Ruth+

Ruth forwarded me the following devotion that quite frankly I did not give much thought to at that time. But looking at it later, it certainly made much sense. What was going on was a severe test of my faith. How I dealt with it and how I emerge from it was important for me as a Christian..

Topic: Are You Being Tested? By Bishop E. Earl Jenkins

"TEST ME, O LORD...EXAMINE MY HEART AND MY MIND." PSALM 26:2 NIV

Let's take a look today at two tests:
1. The offence test. Jesus said, "Offences will come" (Lk 17:1). So be ready! Those who lead always take the worst of the flock. The front line is no place for the weak-willed or the weak-kneed. So, what are you going to do when offences come? Get mad and get nowhere? Get even and get into trouble? Or get over it by practicing forgiveness. "If you hold anything against anyone, forgive him, so that your Father in heaven may forgive you your sins" (Mk 11:25 NIV).
2. The warfare test. This test is for those who claim to be strong in faith, but prove to be weak in fight. "When Pharaoh let the people go, God did not lead them on the road through the Philistine country, though that was shorter. For God said, 'If they face war, they might change their minds and return to Egypt'" (Ex 13:17 NIV). Now, you haven't been called to be insensitive and abrasive, but if

> your destiny is worth pursuing - it's worth fighting for! So, toughen up! It's a battlefield, not a bed of roses. You must engage the enemy each day using each spiritual weapon at your disposal.

If you don't he'll steal every God-given blessing you've got, including your identity, your testimony, your integrity, your family, your calling, and your future. This test demonstrates your ability to continue in your vision even while you're experiencing disappointment and opposition. So remember, the level of attack is the best indicator as to the level of blessing that waits for you beyond the attack!

By the grace of God, I chose to forgive those who had deliberately set out to destroy the ministry I had tirelessly devoted myself to for nearly ten years. On hearing my resolve to forgive them one of my clergy friends called and said "Samson, how can you forgive them so quickly." My answer to my friend was that Jesus has forgiven me quickly. That is not to say that these people are not accountable. They are, but by keeping grudge against them I would only hurt myself.

Pitfalls

Student Reactions

"Episcopal Church closes Barth House" sign

"Save Barth House" sign

The Barth House students felt angry and betrayed by Bishop Johnson's decision to close Barth House. For some, this was their home away from home. The students rightly felt that Bishop Johnson was taking away what was rightly theirs. Some students were unsure where to turn to for help as their only haven at the U of M had been unfairly taken away. Some of these students wrote emails and letters to the bishop. Others called or directly wrote to me. Others made signs and posted them throughout the compound facing Patterson Street. They appealed to Bishop Johnson to reconsider his decision and leave Barth House open.

Wednesday, September 19, 2007
To: Samson Njuguna Gitau
Subject: Join us

Dear Fr. Gitau,

I read the unpleasant news on *The Daily helmsman* yesterday.....

It really did not sound considerate to the users of the Bath house.

I wish the decision may be revised again.

Otherwise I had been looking forward to joining the Wednesday morning prayers but unfortunately I had to work until 5.00 a.m. this morning. I could not wake up early enough to be in school.

We join in prayers for the bath house closing decision to be reconsidered and looking forward to joining in prayers next time.

This is a very good opportunity for people who may not get time to go to church on the weekend like me because of work related schedules.

Otherwise thanks for your email and see you next time.

Yours sincerely,

Marrein

Rachel Robinson's letter to Bishop Johnson captures the students' mood following Bishop Johnson's closure of college ministry at Barth House. Rachel was no ordinary college ministry student. She was the president of the Episcopal Student Organization, as registered with the Students' Organization at the University of Memphis. She was a member of the Barth House choir, lector and actively involved in every kind of student programming at Barth House. Rachel had attended the Diocesan Convention in 2006 and 2007 as a student representative from Barth House. Rachel's letter quoted in full by permission speaks for itself.

September 21, 2007

Dear Bishop Johnson,

I can only assume that this irate letter will be an addition to the already amassed pile on your desk. I understand that you have been at a conference this past week and, I am sure, are disappointed to learn that the fire you started before your absence has not burned away, but has instead, become an inferno. Welcome back.

I believe you underestimated the students at Barth House, in both intelligence and dedication. I have observed you for three years now and while I am impressed with your double talk rhetoric, I can only imagine how much effort you have put into divesting the work of college ministry while keeping up the facade that you truly care about it. Indeed, it is amazing to see the ample Youth Budget passed every year, while our ministry is left scrambling for funds. It is disconcerting, especially to a potential pledging member, that such ministry would be overlooked simply due to personal differences between clergy. Professionalism has clearly been overlooked in this situation, and the image of the Diocese has been compromised. Let us not pretend this is about money and financial constraints on the diocese. I find it disgusting that the report presented at the 2007 Convention has been used to oust a member of your own staff. It was no accident that Fr. Samson's name was left off the list for the three-percent living compensation raise. I suggest that if you have a vendetta against him, you should address it personally instead of making the members of Barth House suffer. You should be advocating God's agenda not your own.

In response to the absurd report published by George Yandell, I believe that members of the dioceses would be interested to know that Mr. Yandell has never been to Barth House or any of the College Ministry Board meetings. I think it would be fair to say that Mr. Yandell has published a biased, not to mention fictitious, report on the services and activities Barth House has to offer. We as a ministry board have taken numerous steps to present factual information but it has intentionally gone unnoticed. The report also includes a Bell Curve of what factors make a college ministry program high-performing. However, this is problematic since the theory of the Bell Curve was debated by the scientific community in 1995 after Random House published *The*

Bell Curve - Intelligence and Class Structure in American Life by Richard J. Herrstein and Charles Murray. The Bell Curve was originally used to argue that there was a link between race and intelligence, not analyzing religious houses on their ministry programs. It is supposed to be used as a means of grading scholastic performance, something Barth House is not in the business of. Maybe if Mrs. Craddock had been aware of that fact beforehand, she could have thought of another way to measure the effectiveness of our college ministry program. However, Mrs. Craddock also believes that financial pressure drives all of us lost college souls to drink in excess, so her analysis is null and void in my opinion. She is completely out of touch with reality and I am surprised that even you would stoop this low to oust a clergy member and a thriving ministry program.

I am a cradle Episcopalian. I was baptized and confirmed in this church and served for nine years as an acolyte. After losing our EYC Adviser, I stepped up to the position of EYC President and revamped our entire youth program. I truly love this church and hope to always be involved in it, but I will not be involved with any under-handed dealings in this diocese. Building or not, the Episcopal Student Organization will continue to thrive because of our spirit and our dedication to the church. I urge you to reconsider your decision about college ministry for the sake of students.

Rachel Robinson.

I have recently seen a commercial where an adult asks a kid whether she wants a pony. The kid says yes and is given a toy pony. The adult asks another kid whether she too wants a pony, to which she says yes and is given a live pony. The first kid looks at the adult with utter dismay and says "but you didn't say if I could get a live one?" To which the adult says "but you didn't ask." The commercial which has to do with the conduct of banks, concludes "even children know when adults hold out on them." The students at Barth House clearly saw how low Bishop Johnson had stooped to get rid of college ministry program and essentially my position. The students clearly saw how Bishop Johnson took a thriving college ministry and destroyed it pretending that financial factors were behind his actions. There is no doubt that he had deliberately held out on me and our college students. The only difference is that the Barth House community and I were loudly asking for a live pony, but Bishop Johnson was adamant in giving us a toy pony.

Parents' Support

A successful college ministry has the support of parents. Parents are happy and proud to know that their children are involved in college ministry. It is reassuring to parents to know that as long as their children are involved in college ministry, chances are they will remain focused in their academic pursuits. Such parents are also acutely aware that college ministry provides and in some cases, complements advice to their young adults preparing them in life. It was not, therefore, surprising that when some parents heard about the closure of Barth House, they reacted with disbelief. Some wrote to the bishop and others to their local clergy asking for intervention to save Barth House. Others simply wrote to support the chaplain in this ordeal. Here is a sample of some of these letters of support.

Wednesday, September 19, 2007
To: Samson Njuguna Gitau
Subject: Hello

Our son, Ben Smith, wrote us about the decision to close Barth House and we wanted to let you know how sorry we are to hear this news. You made a wonderful permanent impact on our son, thanks to your ministry there and we are forever grateful. I believe you are the person who made Law School tolerable for Ben and provided the spiritual grace he needed to mature and accept all that happened during those three arduous years.

Parents place this as a high priority in their feelings for mentors like you, Samson. I recount how immensely appreciative we shall forever hold you in our hearts. But, yours and Ben's is a permanent relationship and for that he shall continue to grow with your help. Please let us know if ever we could be of service. With much gratitude to you and Ms. Lillian,

Love,

Sa and Ravenel

Wednesday, September 19, 2007
To: Samson Njuguna Gitau
Subject: Barth House closing

I wish I could but I have a class at 11:30 that I cannot miss. I do have several friends who plan to attend Sunday service with me, though. Also, my mom and stepdad, who are friends with some of the "higher-ups" at Holy Communion, have said they will make their concern known to the bishop. I'm forwarding you a copy of the email my stepdad sent to Mark Rutenbar, the rector at Holy communion.

I'm not going to take this lying down, I promise.

Good luck and God bless you,

--Cat

To: Mark Rutenbar
Sent: Wed, 19 Sep 2007
Subject: Barth House closing

Good Morning Mark,

As you may already know, the Bishop has decided to close the Barth House on the University of Memphis campus. If this is allowed to happen, the Episcopal Church will not have any presence on a University campus of 20,000 + students and faculty. The information that I have been able to read on this matter is confusing and it seems that this decision may involve issues unrelated to the actual operation and management of this facility. The Bishop has stated that the facility will be closed in two weeks!

I believe it important that the Episcopal Church be represented on this campus with an active ministry. Our daughter, Caitlin, is a student at U of M. The Barth House is a very important part of her campus life. I urge you to thoughtfully consider what The Church of the Holy Communion can do to encourage the Bishop to reconsider this decision. There may be other options for the continued support of this campus ministry that have been overlooked. Perhaps a commission of representatives from the various parishes of the Diocese could be appointed to explore other options. I believe we have an obligation to provide these young adults a spiritual "home away from home". The closing of the Barth House sends the message to these students that they are not important to the Episcopal Church.

I will be happy to help in any way. Thank you for your consideration.

Regards,

John

Colleagues in College Ministry

There is a collegiality of chaplains serving in college ministry. This collegiality is readily experienced when college chaplains gather for retreats and conferences. It is always comforting to share one's ministry with a caring group of colleagues who listen and where necessary, offer positive feedback. College chaplains share an expansive directory whose membership extends throughout the national church. It's tempting to take membership to this group for granted or to value it merely for the once in a while note that one gets on what is going on in a particular chaplain's part of the world. But when one is in a crisis and gets supporting emails from friends and colleagues that one may not even know, one can no longer take this membership for granted. One starts to realize that he/she is not alone. It's always comforting to know that somewhere someone is praying for you and that someone truly cares. Here is a sample of emails from colleagues in college ministry.

Tuesday, September 18, 2007
To: Samson Njuguna Gitau

Subject: Sad news

Samson,

Douglas has just shared with me news of the closing of Barth House on October 1. I am deeply saddened by this development, for what it means for you and for the students and institutions you serve.

Please know that you, your family, and your community are in my thoughts and prayers as you sort out and seek to discern your vocations. Whatever happens, know that you have served well and many have grown in the spiritual garden you have tended and cultivated there. These are the things that transcend the assorted variables of life in this all too human institution called the Church.

Faithfully,

Sam

Tuesday, September 18, 2007
To: Samson Njuguna Gitau
Subject: I am so sorry

Samson,

I am so sorry to hear of the ignorance of the people in your diocese. It feels like more college ministries are disappearing despite the fact that General Convention names it a priority.

As you and your wife have committed to your full glass, I know that the Lord will bless you both as you journey towards that next opportunity he has in store for you.

Blessings and thanks to you for being an example to all.

Eugenie, MSU

Tigers for Christ (Church of Christ College Ministry)

UNiversity of Memphis

Samson,

I can't tell you how distressed I was to read the Helmsman article last week. I hope the situation is not as bad as it seemed from that news. We will pray earnestly that this tide can be turned. Please let us know what else we can do. I know very little about Episcopal/Anglican polity or how the diocese works in terms of outside ministries, so I'm not even sure what to pray for specifically. I await your direction on that.

Thanks,

Tim

The Rev. Dr. Samson N. Gitau

Tuesday, September 18, 2007
To: Samson Njuguna Gitau
Subject: Barth House

Dear Samson,

I'm deeply saddened by this news. Your ministry has been important and vital to the students in Memphis. I remember with fondness many of them who have attended Fall College Conference and, in previous times, Spring College Conference. Far too often, the powers that be don't understand campus ministry for what it really is: a ministry that scatters seeds that bear fruit many years down the road.

You and your family will be in my prayers. I miss seeing you.

Faithfully,

Bill

Bishop Makes About Turn

Following the overwhelming reactions from students, parents and supporters of college ministry, Bishop Johnson reversed himself. At least it seemed so at the time. The following is a copy of the letter that I received from him.

Sunday, September 23, 2007
To: Samson Njuguna Gitau
Cc: Stephanie, et al

Subject: Barth House this week

Pitfalls

Dear Father Gitau:

As you know, I would not agree with your assessment of the temporary situation at Barth House which you categorize as "closing" the ministry. However, so that all will know what I do understand of the agreement I thought we had reached, I want all that you have access to the letter I had provided to the diocesan leadership list on our "Communicator." We will also post this on the diocesan website in order to clarify the situation that is being put in place as of October 1, 2007.

I wish you the best as you seek to find in the course of your fully paid six month sabbatical the next ministry God is calling you to offer on behalf of the Episcopal Church. As I promised, Canon Somodevilla and I will be glad to help you with this search process.

Blessings,

Don E. Johnson,

Bishop of West Tennessee

In light of this letter from Bishop Johnson denying that he had decided to close Barth House, it is important to know what the Bishop had said in his four page letter to me dated September 17 summarizing our conversation and the consequent termination of my position. Here are the relevant excerpts from the letter.

September 17, 2007
Dear Samson,

"Following our meeting today with Canon Somodevilla and my subsequent phone call to you with a revised proposal, I want to put the various elements of these conversations in writing so that both have a record.

First and foremost, I reiterate my admiration for you and the ministry of pastoral care and teaching that you consistently give at Barth House and Immanuel Church, LaGrange. These gifts for ministry are among your strongest, and I anticipate that they will continue to be a hallmark of your priesthood.

"The issue is not your ability as a priest, for you are fine priest. Rather, the issue is whether to continue to financially support a full time ministry at the University of Memphis as it is currently configured, or whether the Diocese should seek alternative ways to do solid campus ministry at Barth House that are more cost effective. I have come to the conclusion that we must seek alternative ways and means."

"Your terminal sabbatical will begin October 1, 2007. As of that date, Barth House programs will be temporarily suspended as we close the doors and establish plans for the restart of the ministry with programs and personnel that are within our financial capabilities and our goals for the future."

"Campus ministry at the University of Memphis will resume. However, we will be taking some time to evaluate our current situation. The needs of students, the cost and style of leadership will inevitably determine the model for ministry we will carry forward. In light of these changes, the role of Barth House advisory board will need to be reviewed. I anticipate calling a meeting of this group once I return from the House of Bishops meeting."

"With the ministry site closed for weekday use, Debbie's job as your assistant will also be coming to a close as of October 1"

"I understand that the arrangement with Judy as your organist is on a per service basis. When I return from the House of Bishop's meeting, let's discuss what seems fair and equitable for her in this transition."

"I trust that my recall of our meeting align with your recollection. If not, please let me know. If you have any questions while I am in New Orleans, please do not hesitate to contact Canon Somodevilla. Thank you."

God's blessing,

The Rt. Rev. Don E. Johnson

CC. Rene, et al

It was evident to me, both from my conversation with Bishop Johnson and his letter that Barth House was closing down in 13 days. In his letter to me the Bishop himself uses the word close several times. It is also evident that the positions of my two assistants and myself had been eliminated effective October 1. It is therefore curious for Bishop Johnson to deny that he had closed Barth House.

But just in case the Bishop's letter has some ambiguity, other things taking place at the same time further attest to what the Bishop had verbally communicated and made apparent in his letter to me. The post office had been directed to redirect all Barth House mail to the Diocesan office. Our two bank accounts had been ordered closed and the funds remitted to the Diocesan office. If indeed Barth House was not closing why go into the trouble of making all these arrangements?

There is no doubt in my mind that the Bishop had made up his mind to terminate college ministry and to sell the Barth House property. The fact is that Bishop Johnson only gave in to mounting pressure, and consequently reversed himself. In this reversal, the Bishop made hasty arrangements to have diocesan clergy volunteer to supply at Barth House for Sunday services. Soon a more permanent solution was put in place. Fr. Terry Street, a curate at St. John's, was hastily recruited. Terry was called to do the first Sunday service of October. What was a one day supply became a permanent position for Fr. Street. My two assistants were also quickly recalled, Judy to play the organ and Debbie to open Barth House for student access over the weekdays! Wow! The assessment was swift!

Unfortunately Fr. Street's heart was not into college ministry. He was a reluctant recruit to a plan he would rather not have been dragged into. In less than one year, Terry had left Barth House for a parish position. A student was asked to serve on a part time basis and have Barth House open when she could be there. In mid February 2009, Rachel was formerly informed that her position had been terminated effective end of February. With that, Barth House had been effectively closed. The Bishop had achieved his goal. In the March 5-7, 2009 Diocesan Convention attended by Presiding Bishop, Katherine Jefferts Schori, as guest speaker, Bishop Johnson finally reported that he had closed college ministry at Barth House. No questions asked.

Chapter Eleven

Barth House is Sold

Justice, hear me –Furies throned in power!"
Oh I can hear the father now
or the mother sob with pain
at the pain's onset…hopeless now,
the house of Justice falls.
(Aeschylus, The Eumenides)

In his letter to the diocesan communicants, Bishop Johnson neglected to tell them that all along, he had planned on selling Barth House to the University of Memphis. As part of his evaluation of Barth House, the Bishop had hired Robert Campbell, a communicant of Holy Communion, to appraise the property. Robert had visited Barth House several times while I was still there. The Bishop had himself told me, both verbally and in writing, about his intentions to dispose Barth House. He insisted that the current location of Barth House is not ideal. It is laughable and utterly incomprehensible that the Bishop would want to relocate Barth House from the corner of Patterson and Watauga to, of all places, St. Columba, about twenty miles away from the U of M.

The Rev. Dr. Samson N. Gitau

One can only wonder whether Yandell's team had found any single college ministry house located twenty miles from the campus. Furthermore, in the spirit of research and good faith, one would hope that the Bishop would care to inquire from the Episcopal students, faculty and staff at the U of M, about the suitability or lack of it, of the present location of Barth House. The whole idea of a college ministry is to provide students a home away from home and not a camp or retreat site, twenty miles away from campus. The college ministry house should be accessible to students living in the dormitories, some of whom have no means of transportation. It begs the question as to why educated members of Bishop and Council and delegates to the Diocesan Convention, would remain silent in this matter.

I couldn't help but see Bishop Johnson as a man on a mission. Since taking office, Bishop Johnson has closed and sold Christ Episcopal Church in South Haven, St. John's Episcopal Church in Martin, Bishop Otey Memorial Church in South Memphis, Christ Episcopal Church in Collierville, and St. Paul's in Frayser and Holy Trinity in Memphis. This last one was sold and leased back to the congregation. Soon Redeemer in Germantown and Trinity in Mason will be history. Watch out Emmanuel in South Memphis, St. Matthew's in Covington, Immanuel Church in Ripley, and Christ Church in Brownsville!

Bishop Johnson has already announced to the diocesan clergy that the diocese is currently in negotiations with the University of Memphis to sell Barth House to them. By the time you read this book, another issue of the *Daily Helmsman* will have read. "BARTH HOUSE SOLD." No, no! There I go again, with

Pitfalls

my assuming trust. I am still deluding myself that there will be anybody who cares enough to even point out the sale of Barth House. There will be none. The Bishop also well knows that people tend to have short memories. In two years, few if any, will remember that Barth House ever existed and that it has served students at the U of M for more than 80 years. Bishop and Council, can you in good conscience allow this to happen? One would think that your primary role is to plant churches and not to sell them.

A close look establishes a pattern with Bishop Johnson. As a candidate, he introduced himself to the diocese as a Cursillita. Cursillitas in the diocese were excited that we had gotten a bishop who cared for the renewal movement. But all that glitters is not gold. Since then, Bishop Johnson has closed the Cursillo organization, the only institution of renewal in the diocese. What is astounding is that there are committees with intelligent persons in the Diocese, but who are much intimidated to point out: "The king is naked."

Rather than seize and create opportunities to harvest where others in their foresight have planted, we must instead sow for the future. Instead of being short-sighted and care only for the present, we must cast our eyes ahead and lay a firm foundation for generations to come. The bishop is called to lead in this role. In my estimation, that is not what Bishop Johnson has done. The Bishop inherited a diocese of 35 congregations. In six years, the bishop has closed and sold six of those churches. That translates into 17% of the diocesan churches. The Diocese of West Tennessee has essentially decommissioned itself from South and North Memphis. At that rate, by the time Bishop Johnson retires, more than 40% of the parishes will be history. To paraphrase Jo Potter's words, "iF THE CHURCH DESERTS OUR COLLEGE CAMPUSES" and I may as well add, and continue to lose churches and membership left and right, "WE'RE IN MORE TROUBLE THAN I'VE THOUGHT." Lord, have mercy upon us! Our goal should not be to impoverish but to leave a place better than we found it.

I am intrigued with Bishop Johnson's double talk. I come from a tradition where the Bishop's word is good for the bank. Not so with Bishop Johnson. In my negotiation with him for my severance package, I insisted that I am entitled to at least, one month salary for every year I have served as college chaplain in the diocese. At first, the Bishop said that six month package was what he could offer. I reminded him that he had approved severance packages for clergy in the diocese for up to twelve months. I should not be treated differently. The bishop finally agreed to look for funds for my nine months severance package. Here is Bishop Johnson's exact wording.

"You have served as college chaplain for nine years. There is no diocesan policy for providing transitional funding for a priest who is leaving one ministry placement without having already accepted a call to another. However, it is not unusual to seek funding for such a transition that would approximate one month for every year of faithful service. I will seek to find an additional three month's funding at the level described above to combine with the six month's package I have guaranteed in order to fully fund a nine-month sabbatical."

Pitfalls

In a letter to me, dated November 11, 2007, in reply to my letter to him, here is what Bishop Johnson said on this issue.

"Dear Father Gitau,

Thank you for your letter of November 20, 2007. In it you state that I have "promised" you at "least a month for every year I have served as college chaplain in this diocese." For the record, again, this "promise" was never made by me and was nothing more than your opinion of what you would like to receive."

Further on in this letter Bishop Johnson again writes:

"Father Gitau, you have been offered six months funding for a terminal sabbatical" by me, and this is what you receive. This is what I promised, and this is all I ever committed to provide."

The bishop's message was clear, "take it or leave it." But when my bishop says that "I will seek to find an additional three months funding at the level described above," I take him at his word. Furthermore, I was not asking for a handout. I was asking for what I am entitled to. Insisting on a live pony, the bishop was deliberately holding up on me and giving me a toy pony. What continues to bother me is how the bishop can claim that his words did not constitute a promise and commitment. My experience has shown me that in dealing with Bishop Johnson, it's a question of semantics, equivalent to the now famous, "it depends on what the meaning of the word is, is." In my case, it depends on what the meaning of the phrase "I will seek to find" is. English majors, please help out! But whereas politicians can and often get away with these kinds of semantic games, clergy in general and bishops in particular, are rightly held to a higher standard. It's expected and rightly so, that when a man of the cloth says something he be held accountable to it. Not so with Bishop Johnson. This particular incident recalled another of several other instances with Bishop Johnson, where he denied what he had plainly said. In this case I had applied for funding from the Church Home Trust to take students on mission trip to Kenya. The Bishop assured me on the face in his office that the funding had been approved. The next time I asked the bishop and reminded him what he had told me, his answer was "But I never gave you a letter to that effect." If gentlemen honor handshake agreements, clergy should do better than that. Whereas it is tempting to play semantic games like politicians, the word of God holds us clergy to a higher level of expectation in our ministry and conduct. It is a genuine expectation that the Bishop in particular, be a person of his/her word. I agonizingly saw Bishop Johnson go back on his word many times. The Apostle James has sound advice for us: "Let your yes be yes and your no be no" (James 5:12).

Unwilling to honor his obligation and accord me my rightful and fair severance package as my diocesan colleagues who have received severance packages from St. George's Church and Grace/St. Luke's, to name a few, the Bishop finally hid himself behind the cloak of the same Bishop and Council that he had used to cut funding on college ministry. Here again is what Bishop

Johnson said in part in his letter to me dated November 13, 2007.

"In a more formal way, I will be presenting your request to the next meeting of the Bishop and Council for the formal action whether or not they wish to extend your terminal sabbatical coverage beyond the six month committed. I will let you know of their decision."

I find it disingenuous that Bishop Johnson would seek approval from Bishop and Council to pay me what was, and still remains duly mine. I have yet to hear Bishop and Council called to approve the severance package of any other clergy person in the Diocese. The Bishop sought an easy way to avoid responsibility by hiding under the cloak of a church committee and use it as a scapegoat. As was to be expected, Bishop and Council did not approve my nine month severance package. In his letter to me, Bishop Johnson said that Bishop and Council was of the opinion that he was very generous to give me a six month severance package. Six months was what he was giving me and six months was what I was to get. End of the matter. I was not in the least surprised. For all practical purposes, this committee was rubber stamping the bishop's bidding. The committee had repeatedly demonstrated lack of independence as a watchdog for the diocese.

I regret to say that throughout this whole experience I found Bishop Johnson disturbingly unreliable. I was ordained in a tradition where the diocesan bishop is father to his clergy. The bishop is the chief pastor to his clergy. The bishop watches for the interests of his clergy.

Some of the clergy may not be the bishop's darlings, but like a parent, the bishop, has an obligation to be an impartial father to each one of them. Here was an entirely new experience for me. Bishop Johnson was adversarial to me throughout this process.

I have tried my best to give Bishop Johnson the benefit of the doubt. For instance, he may truly believe that the parish-based model of college ministry would work in the diocese of West Tennessee. As rector of Christ Church, Chattanooga (1978-86), Don claims that he doubled up as college chaplain at the UT campus. Although he does not detail what kind of ministry he had there, I am persuaded to believe that Christ Church provided an Episcopal presence at UT, Chattanooga. However, whereas the visiting-clergy model of college ministry may have worked at UT, Chattanooga, this does not mean that it would work in any of the colleges in Memphis in particular and in the diocese in general.

Having seen the repeated failure of this model in at least three attempts in the diocese of West Tennessee, one would think that the Bishop would have had the grace to reconsider his determination to push for the parish-based model of college ministry. This model is simply a non-starter in the Diocese of West Tennessee. Neither Grace/St. Luke's, nor St. Mary's Cathedral, nor St. John's have the energy or resolve to currently reach out to students in neighboring colleges. Even other multi-clergy parishes like Calvary and Holy Communion, do not have that kind of resolve. The Bishop should have come to this realization having already met with clergy from these large parishes in the diocese in the summer 2007. Even where this model may have worked, including, Christ Episcopal Church, Chattanooga, reality shows that its durability is contingent on the interests of neighboring rectors and the resources they have to do college ministry. For the record, there has not been any Episcopal college ministry at UT, Chattanooga for years now.

One would argue that if this model really worked, the rector of St. Luke's, Jackson, Tennessee, a former college chaplain, and whose parish is surrounded by no less than four colleges, would be having a thriving college ministry outreach. There currently is none of that. The priorities of his parish are not there. If college ministry is really important to the Church, the Church cannot afford to give it half-hearted support. College ministry deserves the very best, if the Church is to be viable for future generations. College ministry deserves to be assured a line item in the diocesan budget.

Bishop Johnson's persistent push for a parish-based model of college ministry, reminds me of a story of a man born blind. As miracles do happen, the man was healed of his blindness, but only momentarily. When his eyes opened, the man saw a donkey before him. It was the most beautiful creature the man had ever seen. As his eyes closed again, the only picture that remained in the man's mind was the beauty of the donkey. From then on, the beauty of everything and all things was relative to the donkey. The man would say, "is it as beautiful as a donkey?" "Is she as beautiful as a donkey?" It is unfortunate that the man did not have his eyes opened long enough for him to see many other creatures like horses, zebras, giraffes, cats and dogs and their beauty. For him it was always "as beautiful as a donkey."

The Rev. Dr. Samson N. Gitau

Letter to Diocesan Communicants

In the heat of mounting pressure, Bishop Johnson wrote a long letter from New Orleans, to the diocesan communicants. The letter was for immediate release. It was an attempt to cool down the fire he had ignited. Here are the relevant excerpts.

September 20, 2007

"Dear Communicants of The Diocese of West Tennessee,

By now, you have probably heard about my decision to temporarily close Barth House. It appears that many rumors and a great deal of misinformation has been circulating through the Diocese about this decision since it was discussed this week with Fr. Gitau. I would like to have on record that my meeting with Father Gitau on Monday, September 17th and my subsequent letter to him recapping our conversation reflects a different understanding of the consequences of that decision than what you may be hearing."

"There is no question that part of the reason for this temporary closure is financial. For the first six years of Father Gitau's tenure, his full-time ministry as Episcopal Chaplain was totally funded through a private one-time grant. That grant was expended over five years, is now depleted, and since then, the diocesan budget has consistently been able to support only fifty to sixty percent of the cost of this ministry."

"Apart from the financial reason, a research study commissioned by me and conducted by a group of Episcopal campus ministers with recent and extensive campus-based experience, along with professional process consultants, has provided valuable information on the "meaningful differences" consistently in place in successful Episcopal campus ministries in various locations around the country. The findings were shared with the Bishop and Council and with the Annual Convention last February. They were also shared with Father Gitau and members of his board last March. It was against these standards that Barth House's ministry was measured. He was given coaching and the offer of additional coaching to assist in implementing the differences. However, to date, most of the suggestions given to him have not been satisfactorily implemented. (The findings of the research study are available on the diocesan web site at www.episwtn.org.)"

"I remain committed to campus ministry at the University of Memphis and throughout the Diocese. Worship for the student body will be offered on Sunday, October 7th, at Barth House. While I am in New Orleans, I am working with my staff to clarify and announce the times for those services. I am having to do this between meetings here, but it is a priority for me. Local members of the clergy have already agreed to assist me in providing this ongoing campus and in assisting us as we transition into our new model. I anticipate that the new plan of programming and worship will be decided and put in place well before the end of 2007."

"I want to publicly thank Father Gitau for his years of faithful service to the Diocese and to Barth House. As I have said to him repeatedly, he is a fine priest with many gifts for ministry, and he has my support and blessings as he discerns God's call to him for the future."

The Rev. Dr. Samson N. Gitau

In this letter to the diocesan communicants, Bishop Johnson repeatedly uses the phrase "temporarily closed." That was a complete departure from what he had told me personally. More importantly, the bishop says: "I remain committed to campus ministry at the University of Memphis and throughout the Diocese." If indeed Bishop Johnson is committed to college ministry as he says he is, why isn't there even one college ministry program currently operating in any of the many colleges in the diocese? Why has Barth House remained closed for nearly two years? Why hasn't there been any line item for college ministry in the diocesan budget in the past two years? Why is Barth House for sale? Is the Bishop really committed to college ministry or is this yet another example of his double talk? The Bishop tells the communicants of the diocese that an evaluation of Barth House was done. How could it have been done when I repeatedly cried foul on the process involved and even the time line he had himself laid down? How could the Bishop make this claim while all the three members of the College Ministry Board had clearly disagreed with the evaluation report? This is where the Bishop stoops to his lowest. Ten months after the fictitious study had been pretentiously used to cut college ministry financing he openly tells communicants of the diocese that an evaluation had been done. One does not have to be a genius to clearly see an attempt to justify a self-fulfilled prophecy. As Rachel Robinson succinctly puts it: "professionalism has clearly been overlooked in this situation, and the image of the Diocese has been compromised."

Pitfalls

The Bishop references the report conducted by "professionals." This is the most disgraceful and despicable sham of a report I have ever seen. But not so with Bishop Johnson. The Bishop hailed it as "very good," "fascinating," and "valuable," and whose results would have great contribution throughout the state and the nation. Well, if indeed the report was that good, why is it that when my successor was recruited to do college ministry the report was never applied to him? Did Bishop Johnson forget his promise to the diocesan communicants that the new model would be put in place before the end of 2007? It was an insult of my intelligence for Bishop Johnson to tell diocesan communicants that:

"He was given coaching and the offer of additional coaching to assist in implementing the differences. However, to date, most of the suggestions given to him have not been satisfactorily implemented."

It is as if, for Bishop Johnson, college ministry is a mechanical check list. Is this how he did it at UT, Chattanooga? Is this how he was himself evaluated, if ever? If indeed Bishop Johnson cared that much for those meaningful differences, how come he did not invite "the professional" to coach my successor at Barth House? These are glaring examples of double standards. Finally, how come the "very good," "fascinating" and "valuable" report has yet to be heard of again in the Diocese of West Tennessee, let alone in the other two dioceses of Tennessee and the National Church? One reason only. It was a sham of a report not worth the paper it was written on.

The Rev. Dr. Samson N. Gitau

In his attempt to save his face Bishop Johnson posted the results of the so called "evaluation report" in the diocesan website making it available to more than 10,000 communicants of the diocese, but also to many others who would log in the diocesan website. In doing so, Bishop Johnson stooped lower than one would have expected from the holder of his office. He compromised the office of the bishop beyond imaginable propositions. He knowingly trampled on my rights as an employee of the Diocese of West Tennessee. Bishop Johnson was bent on destroying my career while at the same praising me as "a fine priest." He was willing to sacrifice one of his own clergy to cover his behind. The bishop posted the evaluation report knowing fully well that the evaluation process was most flawed. I had repeatedly cried out foul to him regarding this process. He did so in spite of my pleading with him not to do so. He did so knowing only too well that members of the College Board present in the evaluation meeting had unanimously disagreed with the findings presented to him. In so doing, Bishop Johnson knowingly breached my right to confidentiality. The Bishop deliberately misused his office to publicize a false report to the whole Diocese knowing that I had no way of rebutting it. It worked. Bishop Johnson was able to silence dissent against his unjustified actions to close Barth House and to unfairly eliminate my position.

In my letter and email dated September 25, 2007, to Bishop Johnson, I protested his unjustified actions and ultimate attempt to try me in the public arena of the diocese. Here is what I said in part:

"Unfortunately, as I read your email, and the fact that you chose to copy it to all in the list, and also the things that you said to all the communicants of the Diocese, I see an attempt to use the public arena to negotiate my package and to portray an image that bears no resemblance to me and my ministry. Like I said in a hardcopy letter I delivered to your office this morning, I would rather we do not go this route. I am entitled to confidentiality as well as privacy. You are my Bishop and I have treated you with great respect. I intend to continue doing so. You have said that you will put the "meaningful differences report" on the website for all to see. Bishop, you know as I do that the process of that report is flawed from beginning to the end. The three other persons who were with me in that meeting are fully agreed that it nowhere reflects what transpired in that meeting. It is not a mistake that it is signed by a person who was not himself in the meeting. The public display of the report would tarnish my integrity and cause irreparable damage to me and my ministry. I have requested that you do not publish or cause it to be published. Should you go ahead with it, then I reserve my right to defend my integrity and reputation in anyway possible."

I helplessly felt like a person placed on the altar of sacrifice by my own bishop. No amount of pleading to the bishop could make him give a second thought to the harm he was doing to me and my ministry. The Bishop went ahead and publicized the report on the diocesan website. The publication had the desired effect. It swiftly sealed the loss of my job of nearly ten years. It led to the loss of my health insurance. It robbed me of my chances of getting another job in the diocese and in the Episcopal

Church. As I had predicted, it caused irreparable damage to my professional calling and ministry.

At the end of the day I do not feel sorry for myself. Instead, I feel very sorry for Bishop Johnson. I am one of the most industrious clergy in his diocese. I remain a clergy in good standing in the diocese. But in dealing with me Bishop Johnson chose expediency rather than principle. I feel bad for him for not seeing the glaring inconsistency between his words and actions. His rallying call for the diocese is: "Where God's promise in Christ is good news for all people?" Really? Right now it doesn't feel that way either to the many thousands of college students in the diocese or to me. I feel sorry for Bishop Johnson who although he is a member of the national Executive Council Committee on anti-racism he cannot see how his handling of my case is in complete variance to the mandate and duties of that committee. I feel sorry for Bishop Johnson who in choosing the path of expediency has greatly devalued the otherwise honorable office of bishop and highly compromised the image of the Diocese of West Tennessee. In choosing this path, Bishop Johnson has betrayed the trust of many faithful Christians in the Diocese of West Tennessee and beyond, who dearly love this Church and its ministry with young adults.

An Ugly Divorce

Every time a relationship goes sour, one is forced to reflect on what possibly went wrong? I would be the last person to claim that I never rubbed Bishop Johnson the wrong way. I am an independent-minded person that takes my freedom of thought and action seriously. I share these ideals with my students and young adults entrusted to me, encouraging them to be independent thinkers. I am also cognizant of the fact that my actions may sometimes conflict with those of others leading to untold consequences. If and when this happens, this may be the necessary price for my freedom of conscience. However, one would hope that leaders, religious, or otherwise, should be able to agree to disagree and move on with the mission before them. One would also hope that fairness should be paramount in any ensuing debates on matters of importance to our Christian calling and ministry. I, therefore, wish to take a few pages in conclusion, and put into perspective some of the ways I may have made Bishop Johnson uncomfortable.

First, it would be an understatement to say that the infamous 2003 General Convention election of Gene Robinson, the openly gay priest, as Bishop of New Hampshire, caused an earthquake in the Episcopal Church. The after shocks from that spiritual earthquake continue to reverberate in and beyond the Episcopal Church, causing much damage to the Episcopal Church in particular and to the Anglican Communion in general. Cradle Episcopalians who had never known any other Church felt betrayed by their own Church leadership. Many faithful Christians and clergy felt that they could no longer serve the Episcopal Church in good conscience. Priests and their congregations left the Church they once loved. The question for many was where to go. Many left to go anywhere else but the Episcopal Church. The experience was and continues to be, like an ugly divorce victimizing parents and children alike.

Some of the ordained and lay persons wanted to maintain their Anglican tradition. The clergy in this category sought licensing from Evangelical Anglican Provinces in the Global South. Fr. Stephen Carpenter is one of those priests who decided to leave the Episcopal Church right after the General Convention. Stephen was a cradle Episcopalian. His grandfather was an Episcopal Bishop and his father an Episcopal priest. Stephen was ordained in the Diocese of West Tennessee in 1998. He established himself as a fine and hard working priest, who was particularly interested in the education of inner-city children. Stephen was a delegate to the 2003 General Convention from the Diocese of West Tennessee. He was an eye-witness to what had taken place. Stephen came back to Memphis from the General Convention with a heavy heart. He decided to leave the Episcopal Church. He could no longer continue to serve as a priest in the Episcopal Church he had known throughout his life.

When Fr. Carpenter approached me and asked me to help him get licensed in the Anglican Church of Kenya, I did not hesitate to do so. Some of the Christians fleeing the Episcopal Church had already approached Stephen and asked him to help them form a new Anglican congregation. The dilemma for Fr. Carpenter was how to be licensed by an Anglican Bishop in order to operate outside the Episcopal Church. I approached my high school and seminary classmate, Bishop Gideon Githiga, of the Anglican Diocese of Thika and recommended Fr. Stephen Carpenter to him. Fr. Stephen Carpenter was licensed by Bishop Githiga. He formerly planted St.

Peter's Anglican Church in Memphis. Fr. Carpenter had invited me to work with him in the formation of his new Church. I declined to do so. Fr. Stephen Carpenter was inhibited and consequently deposed from the Episcopal Church by Bishop Johnson.

My association with Stephen Carpenter did not go well with Bishop Johnson. On Sunday, November 30, 2003, Fr. Carpenter invited me to supply for him in his new church, then meeting at the corner of Poplar and Massey. I accepted the invitation and supplied for Stephen. I did not find anything contradictory in my decision. After all, I was used to supplying for other clergy friends including non-Episcopalians, when they invited me to do so on Sunday morning. My Sunday services with college students were in the evenings. Word got to Bishop Johnson that I had supplied for Fr. Carpenter in his new Anglican Church. Bishop Johnson raised the issue with me in his office. He told me that he had heard that I had supplied for Fr. Carpenter. He advised me that the next time I was invited do so, "think about it and call him (Bishop) before doing it." I got the Bishop's message. I was not to associate with persons who had left the Episcopal Church. In exercise of my right and freedom of association, I maintained my friendship with Fr. Carpenter but respected the Bishop's advice not to supply for him. I never supplied for Fr. Carpenter or his successors at St. Peter's again.

Meanwhile, Episcopalians continued to flee from the Diocese of West Tennessee just as they were doing everywhere else in the national Church. A large group left St. Luke's Church, Jackson, Tennessee, to form All Saints Anglican Church. The new Church sought affiliation with an Anglican Province. I had known quite a few of these Christians. Their departure from the Diocese was a sad moment. I electronically shared my Sunday sermons with them. I was glad to share with others in need that which God has graciously given me. When Fr. Chuck Filiatreau finally retired from the Diocese he approached me to help him get licensed, I did so. I had served with Chuck in COM for many years. I knew him as a godly priest who took his ministry very seriously. I helped several other priests including Chas Williams, John and Ruth Urban, get licensed in the Anglican Church of Kenya.

My rationale in helping my friends was simple. With or without my help, these orthodox priests were determined to leave the Episcopal Church. They did not need my prodding to do so. My second reason was that the many Episcopalians leaving the diocese needed spiritual leadership. Furthermore, these were our brothers and sisters who felt abandoned by the Church they dearly loved. Maintaining contact with them was the good thing to do. I had argued as much in the Diocesan Convention pointing out that these people needed some follow-up rather than abandonment. When the sheep go astray, the shepherd does not abandon them to their fate. Even more so, the shepherd does not deliberately drive out the sheep. Those leaving the Episcopal Church clearly felt that the Church they loved had abandoned them and embraced a revisionist teaching. On the other hand, some of those remaining behind blamed those leaving for failure to embrace the new teaching. Either way, the shepherd is mandated to go and seek after the lost, whether willfully so or otherwise. I said as much to Bishop Johnson, but my argument did not go very far. Instead, some priests in the diocese were zealously pushing away the orthodox priests. They got their way to the impoverishment of the diocese of West Tennessee.

I have no doubt that Bishop Johnson knew about my help to my orthodox clergy friends. He certainly did not like it. I cannot blame him for that. Many, including my friends and foes, wondered why I helped others but remained in the Episcopal Church. Several principles led me to my decision. First, I have always maintained that "You solve things from within and not from without." There are many who would disagree with my principle. Indeed I will be the first person to admit that this principle is flawed. It assumes that there is a willingness on both sides to seek resolution to the prevailing problem. Those who disagree with the principle would rightly argue that it is presumptuous to continue in an abusive relationship hoping that things would get better. There is some truth to this argument but it is equally true that as long as there is communication, there is a chance for reconciliation. Put another way, any hope for reconciliation must start with some form of communication. I thought then, and continue to think, that the diocesan authorities did, and continue to do themselves more harm than good by cutting communication with Christians leaving the Episcopal Church.

My second principle is from a theological conviction. In my first sermon at Immanuel, LaGrange, after the 2003 General Convention, I preached on Jesus' parable of the wheat and tares (Matthew 13:24-30). The temptation with many of us is to pull out the tares at the earliest chance to do so. But as Jesus rightly pointed out, there is great danger in pulling out the tares before maturity.

The Rev. Dr. Samson N. Gitau

Wheat will be accidentally pulled out in this cleansing process. Of course, there is a lot of finger pointing as to who is wheat and who is the tare. Each one of us would like to convince ourselves that we are the wheat and others are the tares. Jesus' advice is to allow the wheat and the tares to grow together until harvest time. Then, it will be easy to distinguish the wheat from the tares. The wheat will be gathered into the granaries. The tares will be gathered together and burned. I shared my theological conviction with Bishop Johnson and made him know my stand in this major dilemma for many of us in the Church.

My third rationale is also theological. The scripture commands us to preach the gospel in season and out of season. I was called to a ministry with college students. I had the opportunity to do so. Mine was not to try and influence them one way or the other in the raging debate. My responsibility was to preach the truth of the word of God that sets each one of us free from the shackles of sin. Mine was to lead each of my students to own his/her faith. I had the opportunity to do so and I was not about to abandon it. It is because of the same conviction that I accepted requests to help my brothers and sisters at All Saints Anglican Church, Jackson, Tennessee, and Trinity in the Fields, Marion, Arkansas, when the latter broke away from the Church of the Holy Cross, West Memphis. Each of these congregations consists of very fine and God-loving Christians, who deeply care for their faith. I couldn't turn them down when they needed help that is in my ability to give. I am first and foremost a Christian and second, an Anglican priest, serving for these years in the Episcopal Church. In the judgment day, God will not ask me how good an Anglican or Episcopalian priest I was, but how well I kept my faith in helping those in need of help. The price for rendering this help is worth it. There is no doubt I have paid my share of this price and continue to do so. I have no regrets.

My empathy with fleeing Episcopalians and help to my clergy friends which I had no doubt was known to Bishop Johnson, did not go well with him. But if it bothered him, apart from my incident with my supply for Fr. Carpenter, Bishop Johnson did not raise the issue with me again. My prophetic ministry however did not amuse him. In September 2007, I published an article in the *Living Church* Magazine entitled "The Second Betrayal." In this article, I sought to explain how Christians in the Global South have felt betrayed by the Western Church. In their view, the Western Church is going back on the very things they had taught as sinful to Christians in the Global South. I went on to say that the Episcopal Church was trying to stop an unstoppable force. The Anglican Church in North America would continue to gain strength. On reading my article Bishop Johnson called me on the phone and openly told me that he was unhappy with what I had said in that article. Unfortunately, the Bishop did not say what exactly he did not like in my article.

One only needs to peruse the Old Testament to see that not a single true prophet was ever popular with those in power. The reason was simple. What the prophet said about the idolatrous and unjust trends of the nation was a sword in the hearts of the political and religious leaders. The people were also not amused to hear about the punishment that God was going to mete upon them. One just needs to ask the Prophets

The Rev. Dr. Samson N. Gitau

Jeremiah, Ezekiel and Amos, among others, how they were maligned and vilified for their prophecies. Only when their prophecies had come to pass did the people recognize the authenticity of the prophets' messages. Unfortunately, it was often too late. I do not presume to be a prophet but my prediction about the unstoppable earthquake unleashed by the revisionists' trend in the Episcopal Church has taken place and continues to take place. A new Anglican Province in North America is now firmly in place with a new Archbishop. Whereas my help to those leaving the Episcopal Church and my article may have rightly angered Bishop Johnson and possibly expedited the loss of my position as college chaplain in the Diocese of West Tennessee, vendetta has no place in Church ministry especially when it negatively impacts the lives of our young adults. Experience shows that one may kill the messenger, but never the message. The message continues.

References

Aeschylus, "The Eumenides," in <u>The Oresteia,</u> London: Translated by Robert Fagles, Penguin Books, 1979

Joan T. Beifuss, <u>At the River I Stand</u>, 1985

Douglas P. Fry, <u>The Human Potential for Peace,</u> London: Oxford University Press, 2006

http://www.episwtn.org, "Bishop and Council"

http://www.episwtn.org, "College Ministry" - Engaging Students in Episcopal Campus Ministries

http://www.ecusa.anglican.org "Executive Council Committee on Anti-Racism"

Stephen White, <u>College Chaplain</u>, Cleveland: The Pilgrim Press, 2005

Revised Standard Bible

Biography

The Rev. Dr. Samson Gitau has served for ten years as the director of college ministry in the Episcopal Diocese of West Tennessee, establishing college ministry programs at the University of Memphis, Rhodes College, Christian Brothers University and LeMoyne-Owen College. Dr. Gitau is an Anglican priest currently ministering with small churches in the Memphis area. Dr. Gitau is also adjunct professor of religion at the University of Memphis where he teaches a variety of courses on comparative religion, including: Hebrew and Greek legacy, Religions of Abraham and Clash of Cultures. A native of Kenya, the author graduated from St. Paul's United Theological Seminary, Limuru, Kenya, Yale Divinity School, and holds a Ph.D. degree from Boston University. Some of Dr. Gitau's publications include: *One Boat One Destiny, A Study in the Book of Jonah*; *Under the Wings, Reflections in the Book of Ruth*; *Breaking the Shackles: Contemporary Perspectives in Paul's Letter to the Galatians*; in addition to many other articles on religion and contemporary society.